MW00466374

Philosophy of Language

PRINCETON FOUNDATIONS OF CONTEMPORARY PHILOSOPHY

Scott Soames, *Series Editor*

Philosophical Logic by JOHN P. BURGESS

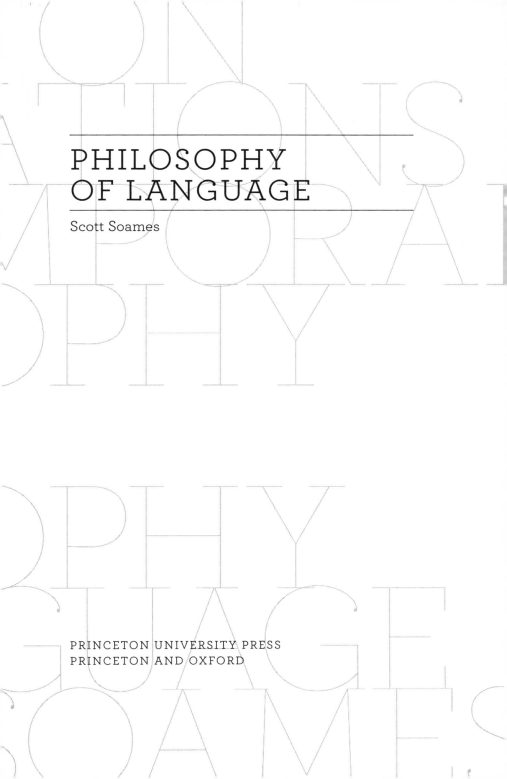

PHILOSOPHY
OF LANGUAGE

Scott Soames

PRINCETON UNIVERSITY PRESS
PRINCETON AND OXFORD

Copyright © 2010 by Princeton University Press
Published by Princeton University Press,
41 William Street, Princeton, New Jersey 08540
In the United Kingdom: Princeton University Press,
6 Oxford Street, Woodstock, Oxfordshire OX20 1TW
press.princeton.edu

Library of Congress Cataloging-in-Publication Data

Soames, Scott.
    Philosophy of language / Scott Soames.
        p.   cm.   (Princeton foundations of contemporary philosophy)
    Includes bibliographical references and index.
    ISBN 978-0-691-13866-4 (cloth : alk. paper)
    1. Language and languages—Philosophy. 2. Meaning
(Philosophy).   I. Title.
    P107.S63 2010
    401—dc22   2010017995

British Library Cataloging-in-Publication Data is available

This book has been composed in Archer & Minion Pro
Printed on acid-free paper. ∞
Printed in the United States of America
10 9 8 7 6 5 4 3 2 1

Contents

Acknowledgments   *ix*

Introduction   1

PART ONE: *A Century of Work in the Philosophy of Language*

CHAPTER ONE
The Logical Study of Language   7
  1.1 Gottlob Frege—Origins of the Modern Enterprise   7
    1.11 Foundations of Philosophical Semantics   7
    1.12 Frege's Distinction between Sense and Reference   8
    1.13 The Compositionality of Sense and Reference   10
    1.14 Frege's Hierarchy of Indirect Senses and
        Referents   13
    1.15 The Semantic Importance of Frege's Platonist
        Epistemology   15
    1.16 Potential Problems and Alternative Analyses   16
    1.17 The Fregean Legacy   20
  1.2 Bertrand Russell: Fundamental Themes   20
    1.21 Quantification, Propositions, and Propositional
        Functions   20
    1.22 Generalized Quantifiers   23
    1.23 Denoting Phrases, Definite Descriptions, and
        Logical Form   24
    1.24 Russell's Theory of Scope   26
    1.25 Thought, Meaning, Acquaintance, and Logically
        Proper Names   28
    1.26 Existence and Negative Existentials   30
  Selected Further Reading   32

CHAPTER TWO
Truth, Interpretation, and Meaning   33
  2.1 The Importance of Tarski   33

Contents

2.11 Truth, Models, and Logical Consequence 33
2.12 The Significance of Tarski for the Philosophy
of Language 38
*2.2 Rudolf Carnap's Embrace of Truth-Theoretic
Semantics* 41
2.3 The Semantic Approach of Donald Davidson 45
Selected Further Reading 49

CHAPTER THREE
Meaning, Modality, and Possible Worlds Semantics 50
3.1 Kripke-Style Possible Worlds Semantics 50
*3.2 Robert Stalnaker and David Lewis
on Counterfactuals* 56
3.3 The Montagovian Vision 63
Selected Further Reading 75

CHAPTER FOUR
Rigid Designation, Direct Reference, and Indexicality 77
4.1 Background 77
*4.2 Kripke on Names, Natural Kind Terms,
and Necessity* 78
4.21 Rigid Designation, Essentialism, and
Nonlinguistic Necessity 78
4.22 The Nondescriptive Semantics of Names 80
4.23 Natural Kind Terms 88
4.24 Kripke's Essentialist Route to the
Necessary Aposteriori 91
4.3 Kaplan on Direct Reference and Indexicality 93
4.31 Significance: The Tension between Logic
and Semantics 93
4.32 The Basic Structure of the Logic of
Demonstratives 94
4.33 Direct Reference and Rigid Designation 97
4.34 'Dthat' and 'Actually' 99
4.35 English Demonstratives vs. 'Dthat'-Rigidified
Descriptions 100
4.36 Final Assessment 104
Selected Further Reading 105

PART TWO: *New Directions*

CHAPTER FIVE
The Metaphysics of Meaning: Propositions and
Possible Worlds 109
   5.1 Loci of Controversy 109
   5.2 Propositions 111
      5.21 Why We Need Them and Why Theories of
         Truth Conditions Can't Provide Them 111
      5.22 Why Traditional Propositions Won't Do 113
      5.23 Toward a Naturalistic Theory of Propositions 116
         5.231 The Deflationary Approach 117
         5.232 The Cognitive-Realist Approach 121
   5.3 Possible World-States 123
      5.31 How to Understand Possible World-States 123
      5.32 The Relationship between Modal and
         Nonmodal Truths 126
      5.33 Our Knowledge of World-States 126
      5.34 Existent and Nonexistent World-States 128
      5.35 The Function of World-States in Our Theories 129
   Selected Further Reading 130

CHAPTER SIX
Apriority, Aposteriority, and Actuality 131
   6.1 Language, Philosophy, and the Modalities 131
   6.2 Apriority and Actuality 132
      6.21 Apriori Knowledge of the Truth of Aposteriori
         Propositions at the Actual World-State 132
      6.22 The Contingent Apriori and the Apriori
         Equivalence of P and the Proposition *That P Is True*
         at @ 134
      6.23 Why Apriority Isn't Closed under Apriori
         Consequence: Two Ways of Knowing @ 135
      6.24 Apriori Truths That Are Known Only
         Aposteriori 136
      6.25 Apriority and Epistemic Possibility 137
      6.26 Are Singular Thoughts Instances of the
         Contingent Apriori? 140
   6.3 'Actually' 142
   Selected Further Reading 143

Contents

CHAPTER SEVEN
The Limits of Meaning   145
  7.1 The Traditional Conception of Meaning, Thought,
    Assertion, and Implicature   145
  7.2 Challenges to the Traditional Conception   147
    7.21 Demonstratives: A Revision of Kaplan   147
    7.22 Incomplete Descriptions, Quantifiers,
      and Context   151
    7.23 Pragmatic Enrichment and Incomplete
      Semantic Contents   155
      7.231 Implicature, Impliciture, and Assertion 155
      7.232 Pervasive Incompleteness? Possessives,
        Compound Nominals, and Temporal Modification 158
  7.3 A New Conception of the Relationship between
    Meaning, Thought, Assertion, and Implicature   163
    7.31 The Guiding Principle   163
    7.32 Demonstratives and Incomplete Descriptions
      Revisited   164
    7.33 Names and Propositional Attitudes   168
  7.4 What Is Meaning? The Distinction between
    Semantics and Pragmatics   171
  Selected Further Reading   173

References   *175*

Index   *187*

Acknowledgments

THE IDEA FOR THIS BOOK, as well as the series of which it is a part, was first expressed in the epilogue to volume 2 of *Philosophical Analysis in the Twentieth Century*, when, voicing my belief that it is a mistake to look for one big, systematic, and unifying picture of philosophy in our era, I characterized what we need as "a collection of more focused pictures, each giving a view of the major developments of related lines of work, and each drawn with an eye to illuminating the larger lessons for work in neighboring subfields" (464). What follows is my own vision of where we have been, where we stand today, and where we are, or should be, going in the philosophy of language. The concrete proposal for the book, and the series, was presented to Ian Malcolm, the philosophy editor of the Princeton University Press, in the spring of 2006 at an APA conference in Portland, Oregon. Since then Ian has been a staunch backer of the project, who has cleared away obstacles and pushed it forward at every step. I couldn't ask for a better editor and publisher. Nor could I ask for a better copyeditor than Princeton's Jodi Beder, who, in addition to doing her normal excellent job, both alerted me to passages requiring clarification, and saved me from several philosophical errors. As for the book itself, I am grateful to Josh Dever and John Burgess for reading and commenting on drafts of specific chapters, and to Kent Bach, Jeff King, Jeff Speaks, and Eduardo Villanueva for reading, and providing extensive comments on, the entire manuscript. I have profited greatly from their help. Most of all, I want to thank my wife Martha for continuing to put up with me through this, as well as my many other, projects. Without her continuing support none of this would have come to fruition.

Introduction

THIS BOOK FOCUSES on two main facets of the philosophy of language: its contribution to the development of a theoretical framework for studying language, and the investigation of foundational concepts—truth, reference, meaning, possibility, propositions, assertion, and implicature—that are needed for this investigation, and important for philosophy as a whole. Part 1 traces major milestones in the development of the theoretical framework for studying the semantic structure of language. Part 2 explores new ways of thinking about what meaning is, and how it is distinguished from aspects of language use.

Philosophy of language is, above all else, the midwife of the scientific study of language, and language use. By *language*, I mean both natural languages like English, and invented languages like those of logic and mathematics. By *language use* I mean its private use in thought, as well as its public use to communicate thoughts. The central fact about language is its representational character. Exceptional cases aside, a meaningful declarative sentence S represents the world as being a certain way. To sincerely accept, or assertively utter, S is to believe, or assert, that the world is the way S represents it to be. Since the representational contents of sentences depend on their grammatical structure and the representational contents of their parts, linguistic meaning is an interconnected system.

In studying it, we exploit the relationship between meaning and truth. For S to be meaningful is for it to represent the world as being a certain way, which is to impose conditions the world must satisfy, if it is to be the way S represents it. Since these are the truth conditions of S, being meaningful involves having truth conditions. Thus, the systematic study of meaning requires a framework for specifying the truth conditions of sentences on the basis of their syntactic structure, and the representational contents of their parts. This framework arose largely from the work of four philosopher-logicians. The first, Gottlob Frege, invented modern symbolic logic, used it to analyze arithmetical concepts, and laid the basis for compositional theories of meaning, reference, and truth conditions. The second was Bertrand Russell, whose analyses of natural language extended Frege's contribution. The third was Alfred Tarski, who both developed theories that derive the truth conditions of all sentences of certain logical languages from specifications of the referents of their parts, and combined these with illuminating definitions of logical truth and consequence. The last, Rudolf Carnap, saw the implications of Tarski's work for the study of meaning, and helped lay the basis for extending it to modal systems. The result was a theoretical framework for the semantic investigation of grammatically simple, but expressively powerful, formal languages into which substantial fragments of natural languages could be translated.

Since Tarski's formal languages lacked key features of natural languages, including context-sensitivity and various forms of *intensionality*, further work was needed. Some constructions—e.g., those involving epistemic, counterfactual, or modal operators— are intensional in that their extensions, or truth values, aren't determined by the reference of their parts. These constructions point to dimensions of meaning beyond reference for subsentential constituents, and truth conditions for sentences, in the sense provided by Tarski. Sensitivity to this led to a recognition that the truth conditions assigned to sentences by his theories are too weak to determine their meanings. While some struggled to find ways around the problem, proponents of *(context-sensitive) intensional logic* showed how to alleviate (though not fully solve) it, by relativizing Tarski-style theories of truth to contexts of utterance and possible states of the world. This approach, widely known as *possible worlds semantics*, was pioneered by a second group of philosopher-logicians led by Saul Kripke, Richard Montague, David Lewis, Robert Stalnaker, and David Kaplan. In addition to providing truth conditions of a more robust sort, the approach expanded the languages amenable to Tarski's techniques to include those incorporating modal concepts expressed by 'necessary', 'possible', 'could', and 'would', temporal concepts expressed by natural-language tenses, and indexical notions expressed by worlds like 'I', 'he', and 'now'. With this enrichment of the framework for studying meaning, it became possible to imagine the day

The Logical Study of Language

1.1 GOTTLOB FREGE—ORIGINS OF THE MODERN ENTERPRISE

1.11 *Foundations of Philosophical Semantics*

Although philosophers have long speculated about language, it wasn't until the late nineteenth century that the philosophy of language emerged as a self-conscious and systematic area of study. Four publications by Gottlob Frege marked this emergence. Two of these—*Begriffsschrift (Concept-Script)* (1879) and *Grundgesetze der Arithmetik (The Basic Laws of Arithmetic)* (1893/1903)—focused on logic and the foundations of mathematics. Their aims were (i) to set out a formalized language and proof procedure sufficient for mathematics, and (ii) to derive arithmetic from the axioms of, and definitions available in, this system—and thereby to provide a logical basis for all of mathematics. Although the degree to which Frege achieved (ii) is a matter of continuing debate, the degree to which he achieved (i) is not. His systems were the starting points for the stunning development of mathematical logic in the twentieth century, and for the use of logical ideas and techniques in the study of natural languages.

Two further classics, "Function and Concept" (1891) and "On Sense and Reference" (1892a), made contributions to both. In the former, Frege uses the key notion of a function to develop the semantics of his logical language. He begins by refining the prevailing mathematical conception, clearly distinguishing functions from expressions that designate them. He then extends the notion to include functions designated by predicate expressions (the arguments of which are objects and the values of which are truth and falsity), functions designated by truth-functional connectives (which map truth values onto truth values), and functions designated by the quantifiers 'for all x . . .' and 'for some x . . .' (which map the functions designated by predicates and formulas onto truth values). In the end, what we have is not just a calculus with a mechanical procedure for proving formulas the antecedent understanding of which is taken for granted, but also a set of concepts interpreting them. With this, Frege laid the groundwork for the systematic study of the relations between syntax and semantics, form and meaning, and proof and truth.

"On Sense and Reference" extends his approach in two ways. First, meaning and reference are distinguished, with compositional principles determining the meanings and referents of sentences, and other compound expressions, from the meanings and referents of their parts. Second, the ideas of logical semantics are applied to natural language. The resulting picture is one in which the central feature of language is how it represents the world. For a declarative sentence S to be meaningful is for it to represent the world as being a certain way, which is to impose conditions the world must satisfy, if it is to be the way S represents it. Since S is *true* iff (i.e., if and only if) the world is the way S represents it to be, these are the *truth conditions* of S. To sincerely accept, or assertively utter, S is (roughly) to believe, or assert, that these conditions are met. Thus, the systematic study of meaning requires the specification of the truth conditions of sentences on the basis of their syntactic structure, and the representational contents of their parts. Frege supplied the rudiments of such a specification.

1.12 *Frege's Distinction between Sense and Reference*

Sentences represent the world because they are made up of words and phrases that stand for objects, events, concepts, and properties. Since meaning is representational, it may seem that what these expressions stand for (refer to) is what they mean. However, this leads to a problem, known as "Frege's puzzle," which led him to distinguish meaning from reference. The puzzle involves explaining why substitution of coreferential terms in a sentence sometimes changes meaning. For example, Frege took it to be obvious that the (a)/(b) sentences in (1–3) mean different things, even though they differ only in the substitution of coreferential terms.

1a. The author of *Life on the Mississippi* was the author of *The Adventures of Tom Sawyer.*
 b. The author of *Life on the Mississippi* was the author of *Life on the Mississippi.*
2a. Mark Twain was the author of *Life on the Mississippi.*
 b. Mark Twain was Mark Twain.
3a. Samuel Clemens was Mark Twain.
 b. Samuel Clemens was Samuel Clemens.

His contention is supported by three facts: (i) one can understand both sentences, and so know what they mean, without taking them to mean the same thing (or agree in truth value), (ii) one who assertively utters (a) would typically be deemed to say, or convey, more than one who assertively utters (b), and (iii) one would standardly use the (a) and (b) sentences in ascriptions, ⌜A believes that S⌝, to report what one took to be different beliefs. If this is sufficient for the sentences to differ in meaning, then T1, T2, and T3 cannot jointly be maintained.

T1. The meaning of a genuine referring expression (singular term) is its referent.
T2. Both singular definite descriptions—i.e., expressions of the form *the F*—and ordinary proper names are genuine referring expressions.
T3. The meaning of a sentence S (or other compound expression E) is a function of its grammatical structure plus the meanings of its parts; thus, substitution of expressions with the same meaning doesn't change the meaning of S (or E).

Frege rejects T1. For him, the meaning of a name is not its bearer, and the meaning of a definite description is not what it denotes. Instead, meaning determines reference. The meaning, or sense, of 'the largest city in California' is something like the property of being a California city larger than all others. Its referent is whatever has this property—Los Angeles. Although different terms with the same sense must have the same referent, terms with the same referents may have different senses, which explains the meaning difference between (a) and (b) in (1) and (2). The explanation is extended to (3) by Frege's contention that, like descriptions, ordinary proper names have senses that determine, but are distinct from, their referents. In the case of names, it is common for different speakers to use the same name to refer to the same thing, even though they associate it with different senses. Frege's examples suggest that he regards the sense of a name n, as used by a speaker s at a time t, to be a condition or property associated with n by s at t, which could, in principle, be expressed by a description. On this view, n (as used by s at t) refers to o iff o is the unique object that has the property associated with n by s. When there is no such object, n is meaningful, but refers to nothing. The meaning (for s at t) of a sentence containing n is the same as the meaning of the corresponding sentence in which the relevant description is substituted for n. Thus, (3a) and (3b) differ in meaning for any speaker who associates 'Mark Twain' and 'Samuel Clemens' with different descriptive senses.

1.13 *The Compositionality of Sense and Reference*

In addition to T2 and T3, Frege also accepts T4 and T5, including its corollaries, T5a and T5b.

> T4. The referent of a compound term E is a function of its grammatical structure, plus the referents of its parts. Substitution of one coreferential term for another in E (e.g., 'Cicero' for 'Tully' in 'the father of Tully') doesn't' change the referent of E. If one term in E fails to refer, then E does too (e.g., 'the successor of the largest prime').
>
> T5. The truth or falsity of a sentence is a function of its structure, plus the referents of its parts.
>
> T5a. Substitution of one coreferential term for another doesn't change the truth value of a sentence. For example, the sentences in the following pairs are either both true or both false.

The author of *Lolita* died in 1977. / The author of *Pnin* died in 1977.

Hesperus is a planet. / Phosphorus is a planet.

$2^{10} > 6^4$. / 1024 is > 2376.

T5b. If one term in a sentence S fails to refer, S lacks a truth value (is neither true nor false). The present king of France is (isn't) bald. / The largest prime number is (isn't) odd.

For Frege, predicates designate concepts, which he takes to be functions that assign the values truth and falsity to objects. For example, 'is bald' designates a function that assigns truth to bald individuals, and falsity to everything else. Quantifiers, such as 'everyone' and 'someone', are higher-order predicates that designate functions that assign truth values to the functions designated by ordinary predicates (and formulas generally). Thus, 'Everyone is bald' is true iff the function $f_{everyone}$—which maps a function g onto the value truth just in case g maps every individual onto truth—maps the function designated by 'is bald' onto truth. A similar analysis applies to 'Someone is bald'. The truth value of a sentence S consisting of a predicate P plus a singular term t is the truth value assigned to the referent of t by the function to which P refers. When t fails to refer, there is no argument, so S has no truth value. This is significant for Frege's account of the negation, since when S lacks a truth value, there is no argument for the truth function designated by the negation operator to operate on, and the negation of S is also truth valueless. The analysis generalizes to many-place predicates and truth-functional connectives. In all such cases, reference failure in one argument place results in the whole sentence being truth valueless.

Sentences that are neither true nor false are not epistemically neutral. Since the norms governing belief and assertion require truth, asserting or believing something that isn't true is incorrect no matter whether the thing asserted or believed is false or truth valueless. Thus, for Frege, there is something wrong about asserting or believing that the present king of France is, or isn't, bald, or that the largest prime number is, or isn't, odd. Though this analysis of negative claims is debatable, it is defensible. By contrast, the claim that (4a) and (4b) are neither true nor false is not.

4a. Either there is no king of France, or *the king of France* is in hiding.
  b. There is a king of France, and *the king of France* is in hiding.

Frege regarded it to be a defect of natural languages—to be rectified in a logically perfect language suitable for science and mathematics—that they contain non-denoting singular terms. Although it is not obvious that this really is a defect, there is no denying that such terms complicate formal proof procedures of the kind that interested Frege. Still, no descriptive analysis of natural language can be correct if it claims that (4a,b) are truth valueless. Thus, something in his semantic analysis must be modified, if it is to be applied to English.

Noticing that the truth value of a sentence (typically) depends on the referents of its parts, Frege subsumed T5 under T4 by holding that sentences refer to truth values. On this picture, the referent (truth value) of a sentence is determined by the referents of its parts, while its meaning (the thought it expresses) is *composed* of the meanings of its parts. Just as the sentence

5. The author of the *Begriffsschrift* was German.

consists of a subject phrase and a predicate, so (ignoring tense) the thought it expresses consists of the sense of the subject (which determines o as referent iff o, and only o, wrote the *Begriffsschrift*), and the sense of the predicate (which determines as referent the function that assigns truth to an individual iff that individual was German, and otherwise assigns falsity).

Being a Platonic realist about senses, Frege accepted the commonplace observations that there is such a thing as *the* meaning of 'is German', and that different speakers who understand this predicate know that it has that meaning. For him, senses, including the thoughts expressed by sentences, are public objects available to different thinkers. There is, for example, one thought—

that the square of the hypotenuse of a right triangle is equal to the sum of the squares of the remaining sides—that is believed by all who believe the Pythagorean theorem. It is this that is preserved in translation, and this that is believed or asserted by agents who sincerely accept, or assertively utter, a sentence synonymous with the one just used to state the theorem. For Frege, thoughts, and their constituents, are abstract objects, imperceptible to the senses, but graspable by the intellect. It is only in relation to these things that our use of language is to be understood.

1.14 *Frege's Hierarchy of Indirect Senses and Referents*

Frege recognized that, given T4, he had to qualify the view that sentences refer to truth values. While correctly applying to many of their occurrences, it doesn't apply to the occurrences of sentences in attitude ascriptions ⌜A asserted/believed/ . . . that S⌝. Suppose that (6a) is true, and so refers to truth.

6a. John believes that $2 + 3 = 5$.

Since '$2 + 3 = 5$' is true, substituting any other true sentence—e.g., 'Frege was German'—for it ought, by T4, to give us another true statement, (6b), of what John believes.

6b. John believes that Frege was German.

But this is absurd. An agent can believe one truth (falsehood) without believing every truth (falsehood). Thus, if the truth values of attitude ascriptions are functions of their grammatical structure, plus the referents of their parts, then the complement clauses of such ascriptions must refer to something other than the truth values of the sentences occurring there.

Frege's solution to this problem is illustrated by (7), in which the putative object of belief is indicated by the italicized noun phrase.

7. John believes *the claim expressed at the top of page 76.*

Since the phrase is not a sentence, its sense is not a thought. Thus, what is said to be believed in (7) must be its referent, rather than its sense. This result is generalized in T6.

T6. The thing said to be believed in an attitude ascription ⌜A believes E⌝ (or similar indirect discourse report) is what the occurrence of E in the ascription (or report) refers to.

Possible values of 'E' include S, ⌜that S⌝, and ⌜the thought/proposition/claim that S⌝. In these cases what is said to be believed is the thought that S expresses. If T6 is correct, this thought is the *referent* of occurrences of S, ⌜that S⌝, and ⌜the thought/proposition/claim that S⌝ in attitude ascriptions (or other indirect discourse reports). Thus, in order to preserve his basic tenets—that meaning is *always* distinct from reference, and that the referent of a compound is *always* compositionally determined from the referents of its parts, Frege was led to T7.

T7. An occurrence of S embedded in an attitude ascription (indirect discourse report) refers not to its truth value, but to the thought S expresses when it isn't embedded. In these cases, an occurrence of S refers to S's ordinary sense. Unembedded occurrences of S refer to the ordinary referent of S—i.e., its truth value.

Here, Frege takes, not expressions, but their *occurrences*, to be semantically fundamental. Unembedded occurrences express "ordinary senses," which determine "ordinary referents." Singly embedded occurrences, like those in (6), express the "indirect senses" of expressions, which determine their ordinary senses as "indirect referents."[1] The process is repeated in (8).

8. Mary said that John believes that *the author of the Begriffsschrift was German.*

Here, the occurrence of the italicized clause, and all the words in it, express doubly indirect senses, which determine, but are distinct from, the singly indirect senses that are their doubly indirect referents. An so on, *ad infinitum.* Thus, Frege ends up attributing to each meaningful unit in the language an infinite hierarchy of distinct senses and referents. But if this is so, how is the language

---

[1] Because they are not embedded, occurrences of the italicized words in (7) have their ordinary, not indirect, referents.

learnable? One who understands 'the author was German' when it occurs in ordinary contexts is not all of a sudden in the dark when encountering it for the first time in an attitude ascription. Rather, the ascription is immediately understood. How, given the hierarchy, can that be? If s is the ordinary sense of an expression E, there will be infinitely many senses that determine s, and so are potential candidates for being the indirect sense of E. How, short of further instruction, could a language learner figure out which was *the* indirect sense of E?

1.15 *The Semantic Importance of Frege's Platonist Epistemology*

An illuminating answer is suggested in Kripke (2008). Someone who understands occurrences of S outside of indirect discourse is *acquainted* with its ordinary sense, OS. Confronted with ⌜A believes that S⌝, he knows that the function denoted by 'believe' must operate on OS, and so, focuses on it. Since thinking about anything requires thinking about it in a certain way, thinking about OS requires him to have such a way of thinking about it on this occasion. That isn't a problem. Since *acquaintance* with something always provides one with a way of thinking about it, he must already have a way of thinking about OS. This is the indirect sense of S, grasp of which allows him to understand ⌜A believes that S⌝. Repeating the story for higher levels of the hierarchy disarms the objection.

Or does it? What Frege needs is not just *an* acquaintance-based indirect sense of S for each agent, but *the* acquaintance-based indirect sense of S. In addition to being the same for every agent, on every occasion, it must *rigidly* present the same customary sense at any counterfactual circumstance as it does at the actual circumstance—i.e., it must, unlike most Fregean senses, present *the same entity* as (indirect) referent (of S), *no matter what the counterfactual circumstance is like*. Acquaintance with physical objects, which does provide information about how they appear on given occasions, doesn't guarantee any such unique and rigid sense by means of which agents think of them. If there is reason to suppose that acquaintance with abstract Fregean senses does provide such a guarantee, neither Frege, nor (to my knowledge) anyone

15

else, has given it. The sense in which the acquaintance-provided indirect sense, IS, of S must determine CS is given by D.

> D. For any possible agents x and y and any possible circumstances Cx and Cy in which x (in Cx) uses IS to think about something, and y does the same in Cy, the same thing—CS—is the sense that is thought about in both cases.

If, as seems plausible, agents who are molecule-for-molecule identical—with qualitatively identical experiences in qualitatively identical environments—don't differ in their Fregean *ways of thinking* of things, then those ways arising from acquaintance with physical objects won't satisfy principles analogous to D (since no matter how such an object may appear, it is possible for a different object to appear the same way). To rely on acquaintance with abstract Fregean senses to differ in this respect from acquaintance with physical objects, is to rely on a mystery.

Although these worries don't disprove Frege's theory, they do illustrate his ambitious Platonist epistemology. It is one thing to use abstract senses to represent what different sentences, assertive utterances, and belief states have in common. It is quite another to take these entities, and our epistemic relations to them, to be causally fundamental in explaining language use. In part 2, I will sketch a modest form of linguistic Platonism that eschews this epistemology. For now, it is enough to note an alternative to Frege's hierarchy that abandons the view that the truth value of a sentence S, and the referent of a compound term T, are *always* functions of their grammatical structure, plus the *referents* of the occurrences of their constituent parts. Instead, the truth value of S, and referent of T, are *sometimes* functions of their grammatical structure plus the *meanings* of their parts.

1.16 *Potential Problems and Alternative Analyses*

The alternative analysis of ⌜A believes that S⌝ is one in which 'that' is a *non-extensional* operator—one the extension (referent) of which is a function that maps something other than the extension of its argument onto the extension of the expression consisting of the operator plus its argument. On this analysis, the function denoted by 'that' maps the *sense* of S onto itself, which is assigned as *referent* of ⌜that S⌝. The extension of 'believe' then maps the referents of A and ⌜that S⌝ onto the truth value of the ascription. Since S, and the expressions in S, retain their ordinary sense and reference, no hierarchy is generated, and sense and reference don't have to be relativized to occurrences of expressions in different linguistic environments. What S and its constituents contribute to the reference of ⌜that S⌝, and the truth value of ⌜A believes that S⌝, are their senses, not their referents.

In addition to avoiding the hierarchy, this non-extensional analysis has advantages for dealing with anaphora and quantification. The former is illustrated by (9).

9a. Mary believes that *Bill* is stupid, but *he* isn't.
　b. *Bill* fooled Mary into thinking that *he* wasn't Bill.

It is natural to take the senses and/or referents of these anaphoric occurrences of 'he' to be the same as that of their antecedents. However, on Frege's analysis, this is problematic. In (9a) the Fregean indirect referent of the antecedent is its ordinary sense s, and its indirect sense is a special way of thinking about s. Since the anaphor occurs outside of indirect discourse, neither its referent nor its sense can be the same as that of its antecedent. Hence, Frege's hierarchy complicates the natural understanding of anaphoric pronouns.

The non-extensional analysis of belief ascriptions avoids this complication. However, (9b) presents a further problem, since assigning 'he' the same Fregean sense as 'Bill' would wrongly report Mary as coming to believe an absurdity—*the-so-and-so isn't the-so-and-so*—and so get the truth conditions wrong, while taking Bill himself to be its sense isn't allowed. For Frege, expressions always contribute *ways of thinking of their referents*, rather than the referents themselves, to the thoughts expressed by sentences. To admit thoughts containing such referents would be a radical change. Presumably, to believe such a thought would be to believe, of an object o, that it has the properties specified by the thought, *where having this belief doesn't require thinking of o in any one specific way*. This would open the door to the possibility of believing *that o is F*, by virtue of thinking of o in way 1, and believing *that o is not F*, by virtue of thinking of o in way 2,

17

while being unable to notice the inconsistency because nothing in these ways shows them to be ways of thinking of the same thing. This violates Frege's central epistemological assumption that the contents of our thoughts, and the meanings of our sentences, are transparent to us.

Although this assumption may seem natural, quantification into attitude ascriptions like (10) can be used to make a case against it.

10. *There is a planet* (Venus), such that [the ancients said, and believed, when they saw *it* in the morning, that *it* was visible only in the morning, and they said, and believed, when they saw *it* in the evening, that *it* was visible only in the evening].

The italicized phrase is a quantifier binding occurrences of 'it' (which functions as a variable). On the standard analysis of quantification, 'There is an x such that . . . x . . .' is true iff there is some object o such that '. . . x . . .' is true when o is assigned as referent of 'x'. Suppose, given this, that we take what a variable contributes to the thought expressed by a sentence containing it to be its referent o (relative to an assignment), and that we take one to believe that thought iff one believes, of o, that it has the properties specified in the thought, *where the belief doesn't require thinking of o in any one specific way*. On these suppositions, the truth of (10) is easily explained.

The statement expressed by (10) is true iff the bracketed clause it contains is true, relative to an assignment A of Venus to 'x', which in turn is true iff the ancients (i) asserted and believed the thought p expressed by 'x is visible only in the morning' relative to A, when they saw Venus in the morning, and (ii) asserted and believed the thought q expressed by 'x is visible only in the evening' relative to A, when they saw Venus in the evening. Here, p is the non-Fregean thought containing Venus that attributes to it the property of being visible only in the morning, while q is the corresponding thought that attributes to it the property of being visible only in the evening. Believing these thoughts (called *singular propositions*) doesn't require thinking of Venus in one particular way. There are, of course, *some* constraints on how one must think of o in order to believe a singular proposition about it. It is not enough to think "the F, whatever it may be . . . ," for absolutely any F that happens to pick out o. However, these constraints leave room for believing one thing about Venus *by virtue of thinking of it in one way,* and believing a different, inconsistent, thing about it *by virtue of thinking of it in another way*—without being able to notice the inconsistency because it is not transparent that the two ways of thinking about Venus are ways of thinking of the same thing. This is what (10) correctly reports. In cases like this, we report agents' attitudes toward objects in a way that abstracts away from the precise manner in which they think about them.

These observations make a *prima facie* case against Frege's transparency assumption. However, the case isn't conclusive. There are Fregean versions of quantifying in (see Kaplan 1968) that mimic the above analysis of (10), at the cost of considerable complexity and unnaturalness. Similar remarks apply to non-Fregean analyses of indexicals, like 'I', 'now', and 'this'. These terms pose two main problems for Frege. First, although their meanings don't change from one use to another, their referents do—thereby challenging the joint identification of linguistic meaning with Fregean sense, and Fregean sense with that which determines reference. Second, attitude ascriptions with indexicals in their complement clauses can be used to make the same sort of case against Fregean transparency made by (10). Imagine Venus overhearing the ancients, and saying: "*When they see me in the morning, they say, and believe, that I am visible only in the morning, but when they see me in the evening, they say, and believe, that I am visible only in the evening.*" Although she speaks truly, the attitudes she attributes to the ancients are inconsistent, without being recognizable by them as such. This suggests that the things reported to be asserted and believed are singular propositions containing the referent, not sense, of her use of 'I'.

The leading ideas behind these observations are brought together in the powerful, non-Fregean semantics for indexicals given in Kaplan (1989a). There, the meanings of indexicals are taken to be functions from contexts of utterance to their referents in those contexts, which are their contributions to the singular propositions expressed by sentences containing them. There are, of course, Fregean alternatives. For example, Frege's own rather sketchy remarks about indexicals in "The Thought" (1918) are sympathetically reconstructed in Kripke (2008). As in the case of quantifying in, however, although a Fregean treatment can be given, the central tenets of his framework seem to cause more problems than they solve.

1.17 *The Fregean Legacy*

Still, Frege's legacy in the philosophy of language has been overwhelmingly positive. He, along with Bertrand Russell, did more than anyone else to create the subject. The development of symbolic logic, the analysis of quantification, the application of logical ideas and techniques to the semantics of natural language, the distinction between sense and reference, the linking of representational content to truth conditions, and the compositional calculation of the contents of compound expressions from the semantic properties of their parts are all due to Frege and Russell. Philosophy of language, as we know it today, would not exist without them.

1.2 BERTRAND RUSSELL: FUNDAMENTAL THEMES

1.21 *Quantification, Propositions, and Propositional Functions*

Although Frege and Russell differ on the details, their fundamental conceptions of quantification are the same: quantified sentences like (11) and (12) express thoughts/propositions that predicate higher-level concepts/properties of lower-level concepts/properties.

> 11a. At least one thing is F
>   b. $\exists x\ Fx$
> 12a. Everything is F
>   b. $\forall x\ Fx$

If F is a formula, (11b) (and hence (11a)) expresses a thought/proposition that predicates *being instantiated* of the concept/property expressed by Fx, while (12b) (and (12a)) expresses a thought/proposition that predicates *being universally instantiated* of it. Russell's word for the meanings of sentences, bearers of truth value, and objects of the attitudes is 'proposition'. Like Frege, he views them as complexes that encode the semantically significant structure of sentences, and the meanings of their parts.[2] He differs from Frege about what those meanings are. The senses in a Fregean thought are never its subject matter, but are abstract ways of thinking of that subject matter. By contrast, Russellian propositions often contain the things they are about, plus the properties and relations predicated of them.

For example, the proposition expressed by $\ulcorner P\ t_1 \ldots t_n \urcorner$ predicates the property or relation P^* (expressed by P) of the n-tuple $<o_1 \ldots o_n>$ of referents of the names or variables $t_1 \ldots t_n$ (relative to an assignment of objects to variables). For now, we may think of this proposition, which "says" of the objects that they stand in the P^* relation, as the ordered pair $<P^*, <o_1 \ldots o_n>>$.[3] If F and G are formulas, and Prop F and Prop G are the propositions they express, $<\text{NEG, Prop F}>$ is the negation of the first, and $<\text{CONJ}, <\text{Prop F, Prop G}>>$ is their conjunction. Though other choices are possible, we will here take NEG to be the property of being not true, while taking CONJ to hold of a pair of propositions iff both are true. Similar remarks hold for disjunctions $\ulcorner A \vee B \urcorner$, material conditionals $\ulcorner A \supset B \urcorner$, and biconditionals $\ulcorner A \leftrightarrow B \urcorner$.

Propositional functions are used to explain quantification. The proposition expressed by (11b) (relative to an assignment A of objects to variables) is the complex $<\text{SOME, g}>$—where g is the propositional function that assigns to each o the proposition expressed by 'Fx' (relative to an assignment A^* that assigns o as referent of 'x', and is otherwise identical to A), and SOME is the property *being "sometimes true"* (i.e., of assigning a true proposition to at least one object). Letting propositional functions stand in for properties, we may take this proposition "to say" that the

---

[2] Since Russell's views about these matters changed markedly over time, I will present one representative set of his views.

[3] In part 2, I will investigate which structures are the best candidates for being propositions.

property *being* $\mathscr{F}$ is instantiated. The proposition expressed by (12b) is <ALL, g>—where g is as before, and ALL is the property "*being always true*" (i.e., of assigning a true proposition to every object). Hence, <ALL, g> can be taken "to say" that *being* $\mathscr{F}$ is universally instantiated.[4]

Although, this story gets the truth conditions of these sentences right, there is something puzzling about it. According to Russell (and Frege), the claim that *being* $\mathscr{F}$ is universally instantiated is *the analysis* of the claim that everything is $\mathscr{F}$. But what is it for *being* $\mathscr{F}$ to be universally instantiated? It is tempting to think that it is just for everything to be $\mathscr{F}$.[5] But we can't use higher-order predication to *analyze* quantification, while also using quantification to *analyze* higher-order predication. And if one must be primitive, shouldn't it be quantification? Perhaps the Frege/Russell *analysis* of quantified propositions should be taken with a grain of salt.[6]

[4] Although propositional functions are ubiquitous in Russell's work on logic and language, it is not always clear precisely what he takes them to be—e.g., formulas, incomplete proposition-like structures corresponding to formulas, or ordinary functions—i.e., mappings from objects to structured propositions. I here opt for the simplest choice, which is the last of these.

[5] Cursive '$\mathscr{F}$', etc. are schematic letters. Roman 'F', etc. are (when used in the text) metalinguistic variables.

[6] The same point can be made without analyzing instantiation away, provided we recognize that for a property to be *universally* instantiated is just for *everything to instantiate it*. Since this is another claim of the form 'everything is G', the Russellian analysis must be applied to it. Thus, (i) the proposition that *everything is* $\mathscr{F}$ is identified with the proposition that *being* $\mathscr{F}$ *is universally instantiated*, which (ii) is identified with the proposition that *everything instantiates being* $\mathscr{F}$, which (iii) is identified with the proposition that *instantiating the property of being* $\mathscr{F}$ *is universally instantiated*, which (iv) is identified with the proposition that *everything instantiates the property of instantiating the property of being* $\mathscr{F}$, which is just the propoposition *instantiating the property of instantiating the property of being* $\mathscr{F}$ *is universally instantiated*, and so on. Since this can't be right, we have reason to doubt the Russellian analysis of universal quantification. See chapter 7 of Soames (2010) for further discussion.

1.22 *Generalized Quantifiers*

Since Frege and Russell were mainly interested in formalizing mathematics, the only quantifiers they needed were '∀x' ('everything') and '∃x' ('something'). When using the system to represent ordinary sentences containing ⌜every/some F⌝, Russell resorted to syntactic ingenuity. ⌜∀x (Fx ⊃ Gx⌝—which translates ⌜Everything is such that if it is F, then it is G⌝—is used to represent ⌜Every F is G⌝, and ⌜∃x (Fx & Gx)⌝—which translates ⌜Something is both F and G⌝—is used to represent ⌜Some F is G⌝. But, this is artifice. If one is *describing* English, rather than *regimenting* its sentences in a system designed for other purposes, one should treat ⌜every F⌝ and ⌜some F⌝ as semantic, as well as syntactic, units. On this analysis, the quantifier phrases in (13) are restricted quantifiers.

13a. Every philosopher is wise / [∀x: Philosopher x] (Wise x)

 b. Some logician is brilliant / [∃x: Logician x] (Brilliant x)

 c. All/many/several/ . . . politicians are honest / [All/ Many/. . . x: Politicians x] (Honest x)

 d. Most students are curious / [Most x: Student x] (Curious x)

There is no difficulty in treating all these cases in the same way: (13a) is true iff *being wise* is instantiated by every philosopher, (13b) is true iff *being brilliant* is instantiated by at least one logician, (13c) is true iff *being honest* is instantiated by all, many, or several, politicians, and (13d) is true iff *being curious* is instantiated by most students. This account of (13d) is not just natural, but required—since one can't get the correct truth conditions by treating 'most' as an unrestricted quantifier (expressing the property of being instantiated by most things), and attaching it either to '(Student x ⊃ Curious x)', or to '(Student x & Curious x)', *or to any other formula*. Since we must treat ⌜most F⌝ as a restricted quantifier (and hence a genuine semantic unit), we should do the same with the other quantifier phrases.

1.23 *Denoting Phrases, Definite Descriptions, and Logical Form*

Russell begins "On Denoting" (1905) with a list of what he calls *denoting phrases*—including 'a man', 'some man', 'every man', 'all men', and 'the present King of France'. He then uses '∀x' and '∃x' to analyze sentences containing them. Some of this is, as I have said, the artifice of regimentation. But some isn't. Recognizing the *definite description* 'the man' as a quantifier phrase, rather than a singular term, is a real insight. As for the *indefinite description,* 'a man', assimilating it to the quantifier phrase 'some (at least one) man' has both pros and cons.

The occurrences of *indefinite descriptions* in (14) are naturally treated as quantificational.

14a. *A man* (some man/at least one man) will meet you.
  b. I saw *a man* (some man/at least one man) in the shadows.

However, occurrences in predicative position don't have natural quantificational counterparts.

14c. John is (isn't) *a* (*some/*at least one) *philosopher.*

Perhaps indefinite descriptions are quantifiers in some linguistic constructions, and predicates in others. A further hint of this comes from Russell's remark that (15b) is the analysis of (15a).

15a. I met *a man.*
  b. ∃x (I met x & x is *human*)

Why the switch from the noun 'man' to the adjective 'human'? Because the latter can occur as a predicate without the indefinite article, of course. Without the switch, Russell's analysis of 'a man' in (15a) would appeal to (15c), which contains the expression he is trying to analyze away.

15c. ∃x (I met x & x is *a man*)

Since not every indefinite description has a corresponding adjective that can replace it following the copula, Russell has no alternative but to analyze (16a) as (16b), or, more properly, (16c).

16a. I saw *a tiger.*

b. ∃x (I saw x & x is *a tiger*)

c. [∃x: x is *a tiger*] (I saw x)</NLT>

This is no problem, if indefinite descriptions can occur both as predicates and as quantifiers.[7]

Russell's analysis of definite descriptions is given by the rule

R1. Ψ (the F) ⟹ ∃x∀y [(Fy ↔ y = x) & Ψx]

for translating a sentence S containing a definite description onto its *logical form*—which, for Russell, is a formula the structure, and the contents of the constituents of which, match the structure, and constituents, of the proposition S expresses. For example, R1 translates (17a) into (17b), which "says" that *there is an individual x such that for any individual y, y wrote Waverley iff y is the very same individual as x, and x is wealthy.*

17a. The author of *Waverley* is wealthy.

b. ∃x∀y [(y authored *Waverley* ↔ y = x) & x is wealthy]

Since for any x, x = x, and for any y other than x, y ≠ x, (17b) makes explicit what (17a) naturally demands—that a single individual wrote *Waverley*, and that that individual is wealthy. Thus, the Russellian analysis assigns the right truth conditions to (17a).

However, there are two surprises. First, the logical structure of (17a) differs sharply from its grammatical structure. Grammatically, it is a subject-predicate sentence; logically it is a multiple quantification of a conjunction, one of the conjuncts of which is a biconditional. Second, although the description is a grammatical constituent of (17a), its meaning isn't a constituent of the proposition expressed, because no constituent of (17b) corresponds to it. Russell put this by saying that definite descriptions are "incomplete symbols" that have "no meaning in isolation." Who would have thought, regarding the first point, that grammatical structure would so thoroughly obscure semantic structure, or, regarding the second, that a meaningful grammatical phrase would, in a quite straightforward sense, have no meaning? Russell drew larger

---

[7] See Fara (2001) for useful discussion.

lessons from these points. From the first, he concluded that systematic analysis was needed to reveal hidden aspects of meaning. From the second, he concluded that sometimes the correct analysis of an expression consists neither in identifying a referent for it, nor in finding a meaning it contributes to propositions, but rather in specifying instructions for translating sentences containing it into other, antecedently understood, sentences that don't.

No matter how much, or how little, truth there may be in these lessons, the analysis of definite descriptions doesn't provide the dramatic support for them that Russell thought. His real insight, as suggested earlier, is that ⌜the F⌝ is a phrase of the same sort as ⌜every/some/several/ . . . F⌝. Although he analyzed these in terms of the simple, unrestricted quantifiers '∀x' and '∃x', they are, in fact, semantically complex, restricted quantifiers. Recognizing this, we may replace his R1 with R2, which, when applied to (17a), gives us the logical form (17c).[8]

R2. Ψ (the F) $\Rightarrow$ [the x: Fx] Ψx
17c. [the x: x authored *Waverley*] x is wealthy

While not changing the truth conditions of (17a), this does change the proposition expressed. Since, for Russell, what (17c) "says" is that *being wealthy* is instantiated by the unique instantiator of *authoring Waverley*, definite descriptions do "have meaning in isolation." However, since they typically occur in what are syntactically the argument positions of predicates, rather than prefixed to clauses containing those predicates, the logical forms resulting from R2 differ somewhat from the grammatical forms of the sentences to which it applies. These differences are significant when the sentence containing the description is logically complex.

1.24 *Russell's Theory of Scope*

One such example is (18a), which Russell would initially represent as (18b).

---

[8] Neale (1993) gives a clear and careful development of descriptions along essentially these lines.

18a. The King of France isn't bald.
  b. ~ (Bald [the king of France])

The description in (18b) occurs as a constituent both of the simple clause consisting of it plus the predicate, and of the larger clause that negates the simple one. Applying R2 to the former, we get the logical form (18c). Applying it to the latter, we get (18d).

18c. ~ [the x: King of France x] Bald x
  d. [the x: King of France x] ~ Bald x

Since (18c) and (18d) have different truth conditions, Russell predicts that (18a) is ambiguous. On the (18d)-reading, it is true iff there is a (single) King of France, but he isn't bald. On the (18c)-reading—which (18a) carries in the discourse "*The King of France isn't bald. There is no King of France*"—it is true iff either there is no (single) King of France, or there is but he isn't bald. On this reading, the description has *small* or *narrow* scope, relative to negation, whereas on the (18d)-reading, it has *large* or *wide* scope.

(19b) and (19c) are the small, and large, scope readings, respectively, of (19a).

19a. John believes that *the man speaking at our seminar today* is a famous logician.
  b. John believes that [the x: Man x & Speaks-at-our-seminar-today x] x is a famous logician
  c. [the x: Man x & Speaks-at-our-seminar-today x] John believes that x is a famous logician

(19b) is true iff John believes the following: that one (and only one) man will speak at our seminar today, and that man is a famous logician. This doesn't require there to be anyone who (really) will speak at the seminar, nor does it require John to believe, of any particular man, that he is a famous logician. By contrast, the truth of (19c) requires both, without requiring John to believe anything about the seminar. The fact that attitude ascriptions really are ambiguous in this way supports Russell's analysis—as does Russell's humorous example.

I have heard of a touchy owner of a yacht, to whom a guest on first seeing it remarked, 'I thought your yacht was larger than it is'; and the owner replied, 'No, my yacht is not larger than it is'.[9]

What the guest really meant was the large-scope reading (20c) of (20a); what the yacht owner pretended to take him to mean is the small-scope reading (20b).[10]

    20a. I thought that the size of your yacht was greater than *the size of your yacht*.

      b. I thought that [the s': s' is the size of your yacht] [the s: s is the size of your yacht] (s' > s)

      c. [the s: s is the size of your yacht] I thought that [the s': s' is the size of your yacht] (s' > s)

1.25 Thought, Meaning, Acquaintance, and Logically Proper Names

Examples (19c) and (20c) can be true only if the agents believe certain *singular propositions*. The truth of (19c) requires the agent to believe the proposition expressed by 'x is a famous logician' relative to an assignment to 'x' of the man m who will be speaking at the seminar, while the truth of (20c) requires the agent to believe the proposition expressed by 'the size of your yacht > s' relative to the assignment to 's' of the actual size s* of the yacht. The former proposition predicates *being a famous logician* of m—who is himself a constituent of the proposition—while the latter predicates, of s* (which is a constituent of the proposition), the property that a given size has when the size of the yacht is larger than it. These points engage one of Russell's central doctrines—that to believe, doubt, or otherwise entertain a proposition p, an agent must be

---

[9] Russell (1905), p. 489.

[10] Unfortunately, Russell muffed the joke, saying "What the guest meant was 'The size that I thought your yacht was is greater than the size your yacht is,'" which, wrongly, requires the guest to have had a specific yacht-size in mind, (and fails to exemplify the difference between a plausible wide, and an absurd narrow, scope reading of a single sentence). See Kripke (2005) for a different analysis, plus a report of Nathan Salmon's view, with which I agree.

acquainted with every constituent of p.[11] Thus, the truth of (19c) and (20c) requires agents to believe the relevant propositions by virtue of being acquainted with m and s*, and predicating the relevant properties of them.

What is acquaintance? On the one hand, Russell must grant that we can be acquainted with other people and physical objects, plus their sizes, if his examples of quantifying into attitude ascriptions are to be true. On the other hand, the internalist epistemology he came to adopt dictated that we are never acquainted with other people or physical objects, and that the only propositions we can entertain are made up exclusively of Platonic properties and relations, other abstract objects, ourselves, and our private experiences. As a result, his epistemology and philosophy of mind clashed with his theory of language and meaning.

Proper names provide a good illustration. Russell was always attracted to the view that to use a name is not to describe an object, but simply to refer to it. Accordingly, he defined a *logically proper name* (an expression that functions logically as a name) to be one *the meaning of which is its referent*. However, his internalist epistemology led him to deny that the words we ordinarily call names are logically proper. To understand his reasoning, start by assuming that when one uses a term t, one can always be sure that *one means something* by t—even if one isn't sure that *what one means* is the same as what others mean, and even if one isn't sure that t really *refers* to anything. Now let N be a logically proper name. If one sincerely means something by it, N *must* mean, and hence *refer* to, something. Since one surely knows what one means, one must also know what N refers to. Thus, the only things that can be referents of logically proper names are objects the existence and identities of which one can't be mistaken about. Since physical objects and other human beings don't satisfy this condition, the only things that can be referents of logically proper names are abstract objects, oneself, and one's own momentary ideas and experiences. Thus, the expressions we ordinarily take to be names of people, places, and (material) things must not be names at all,

---

[11] Russell (1910–11).

and whenever we think or talk about such things, the words we use must *describe*, rather than name, them.

At this point, it is hard not to think that something has gone wrong. Precisely where the error lies is a controversial matter. Here, it is enough to notice how Russell ties his analysis of denoting phrases to his theories of thought and acquaintance. "On Denoting" begins and ends with a paean to the cognitive significance of denoting. We use denoting phrases in *thinking about* things with which we have no epistemic acquaintance. Since, for Russell, this includes other people and the physical world, denoting is needed for us to have any thoughts about the world around us. This accounts for much of the philosophical importance he attaches to his analysis of denoting. Although one can, thanks to denoting, *think about* many things, the actual thoughts one can think are limited to propositions made up of constituents with which one is antecedently acquainted. Since learning a language doesn't extend the reach of the acquaintance relation, it doesn't add to this store of thoughts. This is cognitive and linguistic individualism. For Russell, language is a vehicle for expressing one's thoughts, rather than a social institution participation in which extends one's cognitive reach.

1.26 *Existence and Negative Existentials*

Russell had several reasons for taking the meaning of an ordinary name, for a speaker s, to be a description s was willing to substitute for it. In addition to fitting his doctrines of meaning and acquaintance, and allowing him to adopt a roughly Fregean solution to Frege's Puzzle, it was also part of his solution to the problems posed by negative existentials like (21).

21. Socrates doesn't exist.

Since (21) is true, he reasoned, 'Socrates' doesn't refer to anything. So, if 'Socrates' were a logically proper name, it wouldn't mean anything. But if it didn't mean anything, then (21) would be neither true nor meaningful. Since (21) is both, 'Socrates' isn't a name, but is short for a definite description.

Suppose 'Socrates' is short for 'the teacher of Plato'. Then, (21) means the same as (22a), which Russell would analyze as (22b).

22a. The teacher of Plato doesn't exist.
   b. $\sim\exists x\forall y$ (y taught Plato $\leftrightarrow$ y = x)

What, you may ask, happened to the predicate 'exist' in going from (22a) to (22b)? Since the existence claim is already made by the clause expanding the description, there is no need to add '& x exists' to (22b). Moreover, Russell thought, since existence and nonexistence claims always involve the quantifier, the grammatical predicate 'exist' never functions logically as a predicate. However, he was wrong about this. There is no logical or philosophical problem in treating 'exist' as a predicate.[12] In fact, we need such a predicate in the logical form (22c), of (22a), that results from our revised analysis, R2, of definite descriptions.

22c. $\sim$ [the x: x taught Plato] x exists

This formula is true iff it is not the case that some individual who uniquely instantiates *having taught Plato* makes '*x exists*' true, when assigned as value of 'x'.

Next compare (22) with (23).

23a. The teacher of Plato is dead and so doesn't exist.
   b. $\sim$ [the x: x taught Plato] (x is dead and x exists)
   c. [the x: x taught Plato] (x is dead, and so $\sim$ x exists)

The logical form of (23a) is clearly not (23b), but (23c)—which is true iff some individual who uniquely instantiates *having taught Plato* makes 'x is dead and so $\sim$ x exists' true, when assigned as value of 'x'. For this to be so, the range of the quantifier '[the x: x taught Plato]'—i.e., the range of potential instantiators of *having taught Plato*—must include those who once existed, but no longer do. On this assumption, (22c) and (23c) correctly come out true—since '*x exists*' is false, and '*x is dead and so $\sim$ x exists*' is true, when the nonexistent Socrates is assigned as value of 'x'. This is significant because the meanings of variables, relative to

---

[12] See Salmon (1987).

assignments, are simply the objects assigned to them. But if formulas containing variables can be true, and meaningful, when assigned referents that no longer exist, then the fact that Socrates no longer exists doesn't show that 'Socrates' doesn't refer to him, that the referent of 'Socrates' isn't its meaning, or that (21) can't be both true and meaningful, even if the meaning of 'Socrates' is its referent. In short, Russell's historically influential argument to the contrary is inconclusive.

Selected Further Reading

Beaney, Michael (1996), *Making Sense.*
Dummett, Michael (1973), *Frege's Philosophy of Language.*
Frege, Gottlob (1918), "The Thought."
Kaplan, David (1970), "What Is Russell's Theory of Descriptions?"
—— (1989a), "Demonstratives."
Kripke, Saul (2005), "Russell's Notion of Scope."
—— (2008), "Frege's Theory of Sense and Reference."
Neale, Stephen (1990), *Descriptions.*
Perry, John (1977), "Frege on Demonstratives."
Sainsbury, Mark (1979), *Russell.*
Salmon, Nathan (1987), "Existence."
—— (2005), "On Designating."
Soames, Scott (2005b), "Why Incomplete Descriptions Do Not Defeat Russell's Theory of Descriptions."

Truth, Interpretation, and Meaning

2.1 THE IMPORTANCE OF TARSKI

2.11 *Truth, Models, and Logical Consequence*

In the 1930s, the great logician Alfred Tarski published two articles that became classics. In "The Concept of Truth in Formalized Languages" (1935) he defines truth for formal languages of logic and mathematics. In "On the Concept of Logical Consequence" (1936) he uses that definition to give what is essentially the modern "semantic" (model-theoretic) definition of logical consequence. In addition to their evident significance for logic and metamathematics, these results have come to play an important role in the study of meaning. Since this extrapolation wasn't part of Tarski's original motivation, the genesis of his results is worth rehearsing.

Tarski's interest in truth arose from an interest in the expressive power of mathematical theories, including the *definability* of metatheoretically significant notions in them. For a set s to be definable in L is (roughly) for some formula F(v) of L to be *true* relative to an assignment of members of s, and only members of s, as referents of v. Thus, *definability* is mathematically tractable only if *truth* is. But is truth tractable? The liar paradox, in which a contradiction is derived from seemingly undeniable premises about truth, may seem to suggest that it isn't.

Sentence 1: Sentence 1 is not true.

The Paradox

P1. 'Sentence 1 is not true' is true iff Sentence 1 is not true.
P2. Sentence 1 = 'Sentence 1 is not true'
C. Sentence 1 is true iff Sentence 1 is not true.

Tarski worried that, unless a satisfactory response to the paradox was found, truth couldn't be accepted as a theoretically legitimate notion.

The paradox is generated by (i) the existence of a self-referential sentence that says of itself that it isn't true, and (ii) the correctness of ⌜'S' is true iff S⌝, which seems to be guaranteed by the very meaning of 'true'. Such a biconditional will fail to be true only if S is *true* but the claim that S is true *isn't*, or S *isn't true* but the claim that S is true *is*. Since both are impossible, (ii) seems unassailable. As for (i), self-referentiality is clearly allowed in English, while self-referentiality in formal languages (with the expressive power of arithmetic) is guaranteed by the technique of giving every expression, formula, and sentence a numerical code. In such languages, one can form "self-referential" sentences that "say" of themselves that they have a given property P—e.g., of being provable (or unprovable) in a given system—in the sense that they are true iff their numerical codes are members of the set that codes P. In short, it is not self-referentiality that is paradoxical, but self-referentiality *involving truth*.[1]

Tarski's response to the paradox was to abandon, in logical and metamathematical investigations, the ordinary truth predicates of natural language—which can always be meaningfully applied to sentences containing them—in favor of explicitly defined, but limited, truth predicates that can never be so applied. Let L be an *object language* containing no semantic predicates, and M be a richer *metalanguage* that contains L as a part, plus the means of studying L. Tarski showed how to construct a definition *in M* of a predicate T that applies to all and only the *true sentences of L*. Since T is part of M but not L, no sentence containing it is one to which it applies, and no liar-sentence is constructible in either M or L.

We illustrate with a definition of truth for the first-order *language LA of arithmetic*—the quantifiers of which range over the natural numbers, and the nonlogical vocabulary of which consists of the predicate '=', the name '0', the 1-place function symbol

---

[1] For a discussion of Tarski's views about the paradox, see Soames (1999a), chapters 2 and 5.

'S' (standing for successor), and the 2-place function symbols '+' and '•' (standing for addition and multiplication).

Terms of LA

Any name or variable is a term. If t_1 and t_2 are terms, so are $\ulcorner S(t_1) \urcorner$, $\ulcorner (t_1 + t_2) \urcorner$, and $\ulcorner (t_1 \cdot t_2) \urcorner$. Nothing else is a term. Call '0' and the terms constructed from 'S' and '0' *numerals*.

The Referent of a Variable-Free Term t of LA

If t is '0', then t refers to o iff o is the number zero. If t is $\ulcorner S(t^*) \urcorner$ for some variable-free term t^*, then t refers to o iff o is the successor of the referent of t^*. If t is $\ulcorner (t_1 + t_2) \urcorner$ for variable-free terms t_1 and t_2, then t refers to o iff o is the sum of the referents of t_1 and t_2, while if t is $\ulcorner (t_1 \cdot t_2) \urcorner$, t refers to o iff o is the product of the referents of t_1 and t_2.

The Application of a Predicate P of LA

A predicate P *applies* to a pair <n,m> iff P is '=', and n is the same number as m.

Definition of Truth-in-LA

(i) An atomic sentence $\ulcorner t_1 = t_2 \urcorner$ is true$_{LA}$ iff '=' applies to the pair <n,m> that t_1 and t_2 refer to.

(ii) $\ulcorner \sim Q \urcorner$ is true$_{LA}$ iff Q is not true$_{LA}$. $\ulcorner Q \,\&\, R \urcorner$ is true$_{LA}$ iff Q and R are both true$_{LA}$. Similar clauses are given for $\ulcorner Q \vee R \urcorner$, $\ulcorner Q \supset R \urcorner$, and $\ulcorner Q \leftrightarrow R \urcorner$.

(iii) $\ulcorner \exists v\, Q \urcorner$ is true$_{LA}$ iff there is a number n designated by a numeral $\underline{n}$, such that the sentence Q($\underline{n}$) is true. $\ulcorner \forall v\, Q \urcorner$ is true$_{LA}$ iff for every number n there is a numeral $\underline{n}$ designating n, such that the sentence Q($\underline{n}$) is true. Q($\underline{n}$) is a sentence that arises from the quantified sentence by erasing the quantifier and replacing all free occurrences of v in Q with occurrences of $\underline{n}$.

Tarski required that for each sentence S of LA, an instance of schema T can be derived from the definition of truth-in-LA. Instances arise by replacing 'S*' with a name of S, and replacing 'P' by a sentence of M that paraphrases S.

Tarski's Schema T: S* is true$_{LA}$ iff P

Since we are antecedently justified in accepting every instance of '*If* S* *means that* P, *then* S* *is true iff* P', we know that for every sentence S of LA, S is *true-in-LA* iff S is *true*. Hence, Tarski's defined predicate is coextensive, over LA, with our ordinary truth predicate.

The truth definition is recursive. First, truth is defined for the simplest sentences. Then, the truth of complex sentences is defined in terms of the truth of simpler ones. This works because for each object (number) that LA is used to talk about, there is a variable-free term in LA that designates it. For many languages this is not so. For them, Tarski needed more powerful definitions in which variables are allowed to function as temporary names. Given this, we say that ⌜∃vQ⌝ is true iff there is an object o such that Q(v) is true when v is treated as a temporary name for o—i.e., iff Q(v) is true *relative to an assignment of o to v*. Although executing this idea involves some technical niceties, they don't present any difficulties. The result is a definition of truth rich enough to satisfy Tarski's metamathematical interests.[2]

His proof of the arithmetical indefinability of arithmetical truth is a good example of those interests. The theorem states that there is no formula of LA that is *true of* the set of numbers that code truths of LA. It can be shown that there is a formula ⌜∃y (*Self-Application y,x*⌝ of LA that is true of n,m iff m is the code of formula F in which a single variable v occurs free, and n is the code of the sentence that results from replacing all free occurrences of v in F with the numeral denoting the code of F. (The self-application of F predicates F of its own code.) Now suppose that there is a formula *T(y)* of LA that is true of n iff n is the code of a truth. It will then follow that there is a formula H—⌜∃y (*Self-Application y, x* & ~ *T(y)*)⌝—that is true of m iff m is the code of a formula that isn't true of its own code. Let h* be the numeral that denotes H's code. Then ⌜∃y (*Self-Application y, h** & ~*T(y)*)⌝ "says" (relative to the coding) that a self-application of H

---

[2] See chapter 3 of Soames (1999a).

isn't true. Since this sentence *is* the self-application of H, it "says" of itself that it isn't true. So LA contains a sentence that is true iff it is not true. Since this is contradictory, the supposition that led to this result—namely, that there is a formula of LA that is true of n iff n is the code of a truth of LA—is false. Arithmetical truth is arithmetically indefinable.

Next, we note that for any axiomatizable proof procedure for LA, there is a formula, *Proof x, y*, of LA that is true of n,m iff n is the number coding a proof the last line of which is coded by m. $\ulcorner \exists x\ Proof\ x,\ y \urcorner$ is true of m iff m is the number of a provable sentence. Since the provable sentences are definable in LA, but the truths aren't, the arithmetical truths ≠ the provable sentences. So, if the axioms are true, and the inference rules preserve truth, then some truths aren't provable. This is an elementary form of Gödel's first incompleteness result.[3]

These results illustrate Tarski's interest in truth, and the work to which he put his formal notion. The fruitfulness of his definition is further illustrated by the role it plays in his "semantic" definitions of logical truth and consequence. S is *logically true* iff S is true no matter what nonempty domain of quantification is chosen, or what denotations from the domain are given to the nonlogical symbols of S. C is a *logical consequence* of a set P of sentences iff every choice of a nonempty domain, plus denotations of the nonlogical symbols, that makes the sentences of P true, also makes C true. Let a *model* be any choice of a nonempty domain D plus an assignment of denotations from D to nonlogical symbols. Names are assigned members of D, n-ary predicates are assigned sets of n-tuples of elements of D, and n-ary function symbols f are assigned n-place functions f from n-tuples of members of D into D. The denotation of a term $\ulcorner f\ (t_1 \ldots t_n) \urcorner$ relative to an assignment A of objects in D to variables is defined to be the object that f assigns to the n-tuple of denotations of $t_1 \ldots t_n$, relative to A.

The definition of *truth in a model* is then abstracted from Tarski's definition of truth.

---

[3] For more on the results of the last two paragraphs, see Tarski (1969), and Soames (1999a), pp. 82–86.

Truth in a Model

An atomic formula $\lceil Pt_1 \ldots t_n \rceil$ is true in M, relative to an assignment A, iff the n-tuple of denotations of $t_1 \ldots t_n$ in M, relative to A, is a member of the denotation of P in M.

$\lceil \sim Q \rceil$ is true in M, relative to an assignment A, iff Q is not true in M, relative to A.

$\lceil Q \,\&\, R \rceil$ is true in M, relative to A, iff Q and R are both true in M, relative to A. Similar clauses are given for $\lceil Q \vee R \rceil$, $\lceil Q \supset R \rceil$, and $\lceil Q \leftrightarrow R \rceil$.

$\lceil \exists v\, Q \rceil$ is true in M, relative to an assignment A, iff there is an object o in the domain of M such that Q(v) is true in M, relative to an assignment A* that assigns o to v and is otherwise just like A. $\lceil \forall v\, Q \rceil$ is true in M, relative to A, iff for every object o in the domain of M, Q(v) is true in M, relative to an assignment A* that assigns o to v and is otherwise just like A. Q(v) arises from the quantified formula by erasing the quantifier.

A sentence S is true in a model M iff S is true in M, relative to all assignments of objects of the domain of M to variables.[4]

A *logical truth* is a sentence that is true in all models, and a *logical consequence* of a set P of sentences is a sentence that is true in every model in which all members of P are true. These definitions capture what most logicians and mathematicians take logical truth and consequence to be, and so are good candidates for philosophical analyses of these notions, which is how they are usually treated.[5]

2.12 *The Significance of Tarski for the Philosophy of Language*

Although there is no denying the importance of Tarski's work on truth, its significance for the study of meaning is less clear. His goal was *not* to use our antecedently understood notion of truth

---

[4] The relativization of truth and denotation to assignments, and the relationship between truth relative to an assignment and truth simpliciter, are explained on pp. 75–81 of Soames (1999a).

[5] See the appendix to chapter 4 of Soames (1999a).

to *endow* the sentences of previously uninterpreted systems with truth conditions, and hence meaning. It was to *define* restricted truth predicates for already meaningful, and antecedently understood, formal languages. To this end, he offered not just recursive definitions of the sort given above, but fully explicit definitions— $\forall s$ *(s is true$_L$ iff . . . s . . .)*—in which the formula on the right-hand side gives the content of the formula on the left—thereby rendering the defined truth predicate *eliminable, without loss of content*. He required his definitions to be *free of undefined semantic notions* (such as reference and application), to be constructible from notions already expressible in the object-language L (plus set theory and syntax for L), and to entail an instance of schema T for each sentence of L. This means that the definition of his truth predicate 'T_{LA}' must entail something analogous to (1) for each sentence of LA.

1. '$S(S(0)) \cdot S(S(0)) = S(S(S(S(0))))$' is T_{LA} iff two times two equals four.

Since the definition appeals only to set theory and syntax, one who knows those could come to know that which is expressed by (1), *without knowing anything about its meaning*. Thus, statements of Tarski-truth conditions provide no information about the meanings of sentences. So, if semantics studies meaning, Tarski-truth isn't a semantic notion.

This doesn't diminish the utility of his truth predicate for logical and metamathematical investigations. What it shows is that our ordinary predicate 'is true' differs in meaning from Tarski's formally defined substitute 'T_L', even though the two are provably coextensive, over L. The contrast is brought out by (2a–c).

2a. If 'S' means in L that P, then 'S' is a true sentence of L iff P.
  b. If 'S' means in L that P, then 'S' is T_L iff P.
  c. If 'T_L' is a truth predicate for L (i.e., if it applies to precisely the true sentences of L), then if 'S' means in L that P, then 'S' is T_L iff P.

The connection between meaning and truth is reflected in the obviousness of (2a). If, prior to learning the meaning of S, we are told that S is *true* in L iff two times two is four, we can

39

immediately conclude that S *doesn't mean* in L that two times two isn't four—since if it did, we would have both that S is true iff two times two is four, and (by (2a)) that S is true iff two times two isn't four, which is contradictory. The apriori availability of (2a) for inferences of this sort is what allows statements of truth conditions to provide information about meaning. By contrast, instances of (2b) aren't obvious. Because of this, one can know both (1) and the definition of 'T_{LA}', and still *not* have enough information to conclude that the sentence mentioned in (1) *doesn't mean* that two times two *isn't* four. Tarski wouldn't, of course, count 'T_L' as a truth predicate, unless ⌜'S' is T_L⌝ were materially equivalent to any metalanguage paraphrase P of S.[6] Thus, he takes (2c) to be obvious. However, this is not enough to allow us to derive information about meaning from ⌜'S' is T_L iff P⌝, or to make Tarski-truth a semantic notion.[7]

Although these conclusions are consistent with Tarski (1935) and (1936), they are inconsistent with certain remarks in his later philosophical writing. For example, in explaining his truth definition to nonspecialists in Tarski (1969), he describes instances of schema T—like "'Snow is white' is true (in English) iff snow is white"—as "partial definitions" that give the meaning of the ordinary predicate 'true' as applied to particular sentences. Because of this, he took a general definition that entails a "partial definition" for each sentence of L to be one that *captures the meaning* of our ordinary truth predicate (restricted to L).[8] This, I suspect, is what prompts the remark that his definition "does not aim to specify the meaning of a familiar word used to denote a novel notion; on the contrary, it aims to catch hold of the actual meaning of an old

---

[6] In (2) 'S' and 'P' are used as schematic letters. In the paragraph they are metalinguistic variables.

[7] One can know that which is stated by the Tarskian definition without knowing the meanings of L's sentences, and so without knowing that the definition is materially adequate and thus introduces a predicate that applies to all and only the true sentences of L. One in this position has no way of knowing the relevant instances of (2b). For discussion, see Soames (1984), section III, and Soames (1999a), pp. 102–7.

[8] Tarski (1969), p. 64.

notion."[9] Since he took his definition to be successful, he naturally thought that his defined truth predicate could play all legitimate theoretical roles for which we need a notion of truth for L. Since our ordinary notion of truth *is* central to semantics, it is therefore not surprising that he should (wrongly) say, following Carnap (1942), that *his notion of truth* can be used to define the central concepts of the theory of meaning.[10]

2.2 Rudolf Carnap's Embrace of Truth-Theoretic Semantics

This error is already present in Carnap (1936), which was delivered at a philosophical congress in 1935, at which Tarski also spoke about his new "semantics." Carnap's main point—that truth and confirmation must be sharply distinguished—was a much needed corrective to prevailing views among leading logical empiricists. However, his argument for this correct conclusion suffered from the mistaken idea that corresponding instances of the schemata in (3), as well as those in (4), have essentially the same content.[11]

3. S / 'S' is true (in L) / 'S' is T_L ('T_L' is Tarski's truth predicate.)

4. John knows that S / John knows that 'S' is true (in L) / John knows that 'S' is T_L

They do not. Let us accept, for the sake of argument, his idea that necessarily, analytically, and apriori equivalent sentences "have the same content." Then, since S and $\ulcorner$'S' is $T_L$$\urcorner$ are so equivalent, their contents can be identified, as can the contents of $\ulcorner$John knows that S$\urcorner$ and $\ulcorner$John knows that 'S' is $T_L$$\urcorner$. However, this is not true of S and $\ulcorner$'S' is true (in L)$\urcorner$, or of $\ulcorner$John knows that S$\urcorner$ and $\ulcorner$John knows that 'S' is true (in L)$\urcorner$. For example, if John doesn't

---

[9] Tarski (1944), p. 341.

[10] Ibid., section 13.

[11] Carnap (1936), see pp. 120–21 of the 1949 English translation, in Feigl and Sellars. Whereas 'S' is a schematic letter in (3) and (4), it is a metalinguistic variable in this paragraph.

understand English, he may know that the earth is round without knowing that 'the earth is round' is a true sentence (of English).[12] The failure to see this is ironic for a theorist like Carnap, who believed that knowledge of truth conditions provides information about meaning. For surely, if—like ⌜'S' is T_L⌝—⌜'S' is true (in L)⌝ were equivalent to, and hence had essentially the same content as, S, then ⌜'S' is true (in L) iff S⌝ would—like ⌜'S' is T_L iff S⌝—be equivalent to, and hence have essentially the same content as, ⌜S iff S⌝. But then, since knowledge of that expressed by the latter provides *no information about meaning*, knowledge of that expressed by the former wouldn't either. Thus, one who takes knowledge of truth conditions to provide such information must be careful to distinguish truth from Tarski-truth.

Carnap fails to do this in his otherwise path-breaking *Introduction to Semantics* (1942) --where he systematically lays out the idea that a previously uninterpreted language can be given an interpretation by assigning designations to its nonlogical vocabulary, and truth conditions to its sentences, while the meanings of the sentences of an already meaningful language can be described by identifying designations, and specifying truth conditions. Where he goes wrong is in characterizing the Tarski-like rules for designation and truth as *definitions* of these concepts.[13] Fortunately, this error is easily corrected. *If* our ordinary notions of truth and designation are nonparadoxical and theoretically legitimate, they can be used in Tarski-style rules to state truth and designation conditions that provide genuine information about meanings. The requirement (adapted from Tarski's condition of material adequacy, and implicit in Carnap's discussion) that for each sentence S of L, the rules of a semantic theory entail a theorem ⌜'S' is true in L iff P⌝, where P means the same as S, ensures

---

[12] These points about equivalence and nonequivalence are explained on pp. 370–71 of Soames (2003c).

[13] See in particular sections 4, 5, and 7 of Carnap (1942). In contrast to Carnap, Alonzo Church recognized that Tarski's notion of truth is a not genuinely semantic notion. See Church (1944), pp. 65–66.

that the theory assigns every sentence correct and natural truth conditions, along the lines of

5. '$S(S(0)) \cdot S(S(0)) = S(S(S(S(0))))$' is true in LA iff two times two equals four

on the basis of an interpretation of its semantically significant parts. Although—as we shall soon see—satisfying this requirement is not *sufficient* to identify the meanings of sentences, or to understand them, one can appreciate why it might be thought *necessary* for these tasks, and also why one might be optimistic that a theory of truth conditions would prove to be a central part of an adequate theory of meaning.

In addition to generating claims about truth conditions, Carnap's semantic theory delivers claims about analyticity—labeled *logical truth*—and synonymy—labeled *logical equivalence*. These ideas are refined and extended in *Meaning and Necessity* (1947), where he introduces *state-descriptions*. Though intended as stand-ins for possible world-states, they are essentially models in which a complete assignment of truth values to atomic sentences is sufficient for evaluating all object-language sentences (since all objects are assumed to be named). The work contains two main advances. The first is "the method of intension and extension," which is contrasted with Frege's "method of sense and reference." *The extension* of a singular term at a state description D is its referent at D, the extension of a predicate at D is the set of things it applies to at D, and the extension of a sentence at D is its truth value at D. *Intensions* are functions from state descriptions to extensions. Intension is (roughly) the replacement for Fregean sense. The intension of a singular term is called an *individual concept*, the intension of a predicate is called a *property*, and the intension of a sentence is called a *proposition*. Carnap's innovation is to define these notions in terms of truth and designation, and to integrate them into a formal semantic theory that is, at base, a theory of truth conditions.

The price of this innovation is a coarse-grained conception of properties and propositions in which logically (i.e., analytically) equivalent predicates express the same properties, and logically (analytically) equivalent sentences express the same propositions. Since Carnap identifies necessity with analyticity, this means that necessarily equivalent sentences "say" the same thing. However, he doesn't want all necessary truths to turn out synonymous. Thus, he introduces the notion *intensional isomorphism*, according to which two compound expressions are intensionally isomorphic iff they are constructed in the same way from constituents with the same intensions. This is his account of synonymy. Although not without appeal, the account is subject to certain Fregean objections.[14] On the other hand, he avoids certain problems by introducing *intensional operators*, the extensions of which are functions that assign extensions to the *intensions* of their arguments. By allowing such operators, Carnap avoids the hierarchy of indirect senses and references, and the relativization of sense and reference to *occurrences* of expressions, which are consequences of Frege's insistence that the reference (extension) of the whole must always be a function of the reference (extension) of the parts.

The second main advance of Carnap (1947) is the semantic treatment given to the modal notions 'it is necessary/possible that', which are introduced as intensional operators in his object language. The possibility operator is seen as assigning truth to those sentential intensions that assign truth to at least one state description, while the necessity operator assigns truth to intensions that assign truth to all state descriptions. Roughly put, possibility is truth at some possible world-state, and necessity is truth at all such states. Carnap's formal treatment of these ideas helped lay the groundwork for future work on intensional logic and possible worlds semantics. However, with his conception of necessity as analyticity, and the accompanying picture of state-descriptions as essentially models for interpreting a language that respect meaning postulates governing conceptual relationships among the nonlogical vocabulary, his system is a halfway house in the journey from standard, extensional systems, and their Tarskian models, to richer systems incorporating genuinely possible *ways the world could have been*, and the accompanying nonlinguistic accounts of necessity and possibility.

---

[14] See Church (1954).

2.3 THE SEMANTIC APPROACH OF DONALD DAVIDSON

The Carnapian idea that Tarski-style rules can be used to *endow* an uninterpreted formal language with meaning, and also to *describe* the semantic structure of a language already in use, was applied to natural language in Donald Davidson (1967). The chief *technical* goal of the program was to identify logical forms of English sentences that could be used to derive the truth conditions of those sentences from axioms interpreting their semantically relevant parts. The chief *philosophical* goal was to justify the claim that completing this task would yield a theory of meaning. Optimism that these goals could be met was fueled by the attractiveness of the overall picture, which was seen as applying advances in philosophical logic to the interpretation of natural language, without backsliding on W. V. Quine's then influential skepticism about meaning.[15] Davidson held that systematic knowledge of truth and reference could do all the work for which we need a notion of meaning. His strategy was to embrace Quine's rejection of analyticity, synonymy, and our ordinary notion of meaning, substituting knowledge of truth and reference whenever there was something genuine to be captured. Since these notions are scientifically legitimate, the theory was deemed respectable. Its aim of explaining linguistic competence also fit the emerging paradigm in linguistics—raising the intriguing possibility that his hidden logical forms might turn out to be Chomskian deep structures.[16]

Initially, Davidson, like Carnap, wrongly took Tarski-truth to be the notion he needed. He was also a revisionist about reference, denying that referential axioms of truth theories state genuine facts about the world.[17] Instead, he took their contents to be inherited from the fact-stating theorems about truth conditions they are used to derive. One derives the truth conditions of S from axioms about the reference of S's parts, which are used in deriving the truth conditions of other sentences containing those parts. Since many of these sentences contain words not in S, further

[15] Quine (1951, 1960).
[16] Chomsky (1965), Harman (1972).
[17] Davidson (1977).

referential axioms are needed to derive theorems stating their truth conditions, thereby linking their interpretations to that of S. And so it goes, until the contents of every sentence and word are intertwined with, and dependent upon, the contents of every other. In the end, Davidson thought, understanding any word or sentence is conceptually dependent on understanding every other word and sentence—a radical version of meaning holism, akin to Quine's own.

This was the philosophical canvas on which Davidson painted. Some of his main theses, like the idea that Tarski-truth can be used for his purposes, were errors to be recanted.[18] Others—including Quine's critique of analyticity, synonymy, and meaning—are open to powerful objections.[19] Fortunately, most of this philosophical baggage has now fallen away, leaving us free to tackle the key question for the Davidsonian program on its own. How, if at all, can one justify the claim that theories of truth qualify as theories of meaning?

Davidson originally held that a truth theory for L is a theory of meaning, if knowledge of what it states is sufficient for understanding L. The problem was in showing that his theories satisfied the condition. How can knowledge of a theory be sufficient for understanding meaning, when its theorems give truth conditions only in the weak sense of pairing sentences with materially equivalent claims? If all one knows about S is given by ⌜'S' is true iff P⌝, one can readily draw the negative conclusion expressed by ⌜S doesn't mean that ~P⌝. But how does one reach a positive conclusion about what S does mean? Initially, Davidson thought that compositionality was the answer. In compositional theories, the truth conditions of sentences are derived from axioms interpreting their parts. Thus, he reasoned, "accidentally true" statements of truth conditions, like *'Snow is white' is true iff grass is green,* won't be generated without also generating falsehoods, like *'Snow is grass' is true iff grass is grass* and *'Trees are green' is true iff trees*

---

[18] See Soames (1984), pp. 422–24, Soames (1999a), pp. 102–7, and Davidson (1990).

[19] Chapters 16–17 of Soames (2003a), section iv of Soames (1999b), and chapters 11–12 of Soames (2003b).

are white. Instead, he thought, truth theories that are true and compositional will derive only those statements $\ulcorner$'S' is true iff P$\urcorner$ in which P is a close enough paraphrase of S that "nothing essential to the idea of meaning . . . [will remain] to be captured."[20]

Foster (1976) showed him to be wrong. Let L_s be an extensional fragment of Spanish, and T1 be a compositional theory that delivers a *translational T-theorem*—$\ulcorner$'S' is true in L_s iff P$\urcorner$ in which P means the same as S—for each sentence of L_s. Form T2 by replacing all axioms of T1 interpreting an expression, or construction, with new axioms stating different, but extensionally equivalent, interpretations. Since T1 is compositional and true, so is T2—despite the fact that *all* T-theorems of T2 may, like (6), be nontranslational.

6. 'El libro es verde' is true in L_s iff the book is green and first-order arithmetic is incomplete.

Since knowledge of these theorems isn't sufficient to understand L_s, T2 can't be a theory of meaning, despite satisfying Davidson's constraints. The problem remains, even if we adopt constraints strong enough to rule out all but *translational truth theories* (which entail a translational T-theorem for each sentence). Knowing that which is stated by the translational T1 is no more useful in coming to understand L_s than knowing what is stated by the nontranslational T2, *unless one also knows, of that stated by T1, that it is expressed by a translational theory*. If one wrongly takes T1 to be nontranslational, then knowledge of the truth conditions it states won't yield knowledge of meaning. Thus, knowledge of what is stated by even the best truth theories is insufficient for understanding meaning.

Davidson (1976) responds with the obvious minimal revision of his original justificatory proposal. On the revised view, what makes a translational truth theory T a correct theory of meaning is that knowledge of the claim made by the conjunction of its axioms, *plus* knowledge, of that claim, that it is made by a translational theory, are, together, sufficient for understanding.

---

[20] Davidson (1967), p. 26 of the 2001 reprinting. Italics in the above paragraph in the text is used as a device of quotation.

Knowledge of the axioms allows one to derive a truth theorem for each S that pairs S with *the claim expressed by a translation of S*; knowledge, of this truth-conditional knowledge, that it is expressed by a translational theory, allows one to identify that claim as *the claim expressed by S*, and thus to understand S. However, as shown in Soames (1992), this reasoning fails. For each S, T entails infinitely many theorems ⌜'S' is true iff P⌝. Although one is translational, nothing in T specifies which one. Since knowledge of a theory known to be translational doesn't allow one to separate translational from nontranslational theorems, it *doesn't* suffice for understanding L.

The natural response is to add a definition of *canonical theorem* to truth theories, picking out, for each S, a unique theorem CT as translational. However, it is doubtful that even this would provide the needed justification. Once this information is added, knowledge of T allows one to identify a claim that pairs S with its content. However, neither the truth of CT, nor the fact that it states truth conditions, play any role in interpreting S. All CT does is supply a translational pairing that could be supplied equally well in other ways. One could get the same interpretive results by replacing the truth predicate in a translational truth theory with any predicate F. Whether or not the resulting theory is true makes no difference. To interpret S, all one needs to know, of the canonical F-theorem, is that it links S with its content. Surely, this doesn't justify taking translational F-theories to be theories of meaning. Since a similar point holds for truth theories, we still have no solution to Davidson's justification problem.

Some believe that the solution is psychological. For a theory of truth *cum* theory of meaning to be correct is, they say, for speakers to use it unconsciously to interpret sentences, with canonical T-theorems terminating the derivations of speakers.[21] In addition to being unsupported by evidence, however, such psycholinguistic speculation is implausible—requiring, as it does, an incredibly rich "language of thought" needed to state the truth conditions of all natural language sentences. It is also confused. The only *psychological* use to which it puts the truth theory is that of con-

[21] See Larson and Segal (1995).

necting English sentences with Mentalese translations. But if this were what understanding amounted to, more efficient and direct methods of translation could easily be found. Finally, even if, by purest luck, existing speakers did use internalized truth theories as imagined, this wouldn't be a semantic fact about English, but a psychological quirk about them. A new speaker who assigned English sentences the same interpretations they do, but used a different method for translating into Mentalese, would still speak English. Thus, Davidson's semantic program can't be saved by psychologizing it.

To date, no solution has been found to the program's justification problem.[22] Although there is much to be learned from its application of the techniques of philosophical logic to natural language, there are, as yet, no grounds for taking the resulting truth theories to be theories of meaning.

Selected Further Reading

Carnap, Rudolf (1947), *Meaning and Necessity.*
———— (1949), "Truth and Confirmation."
Davidson, Donald (2001), *Inquiries into Truth and Interpretation.*
Etchemendy, John (1988), "Tarski on Truth and Logical Consequence."
Field, Hartry (1972), "Tarski's Theory of Truth." *Journal of Philosophy* 69, 347–75.
Gomez-Torrente, Mario (1996), "Tarski on Logical Consequence."
Lepore, Ernest, and Ludwig, Kirk (2007), *Donald Davidson: Meaning, Truth, Language and Reality.*
———— (2009), *Donald Davidson's Truth-Theoretic Semantics.*
Soames, Scott (1999a), *Understanding Truth*, chapters 3–5.
———— (2008a), "Truth and Meaning: in Perspective."
Tarski, Alfred (1969), "Truth and Proof."

---

[22] The most promising recent attempted solution, in Higginbotham (1992), is refuted in Soames (2008a).

Meaning, Modality, and Possible Worlds Semantics

3.1 Kripke-Style Possible Worlds Semantics

Whereas Davidsonians apply semantic ideas from *extensional logic* to natural language, possible worlds semanticists apply similar ideas from *modal logic*. The initial aim of these systems was to introduce an operator '□' into languages of the predicate calculus with roughly the meaning "it is a logical/analytic/necessary truth that"—so that prefixing it to a standard logical truth would produce a truth. Since the operator can be iterated, the resulting logic is more complex than that. However, apart from persistent problems of interpretation—*What is this notion of logical/analytic/ necessary truth that is to be captured?*—the underlying technical ideas are clear. Since modal operators express operators defined in terms of truth at *model-like* elements, *models* for modal languages must contain such elements—typically (but misleadingly) called "possible worlds." These are the elements relative to which quantifiers have domains, expressions have extensions, and sentences have truth values. A model for a modal language L_M consists of (i) a nonempty set W of "possible worlds," (ii) a relation R on W, relating w_1 to w_2 iff w_2 is "possible"/"accessible" from w_1, (iii) a designated member @ of W called "the actual world," (iv) a nonempty set I of "possible individuals," and an assignment, to each w of W, of a subset of I as the domain of quantification for w, and (v) a valuation function assigning an *intension* to each nonlogical symbol, which maps each member w of W to its extension at w.

Truth at a world w in a model M, and *logical truth*, are defined as follows:

Truth at a World in a Model

⌜$Pt_1 \ldots t_n$⌝ is true at w in M, relative to an assignment A (of objects to variables), iff the n-tuple of denotations (extensions) of $t_1 \ldots t_n$ at w in M, relative to A, is a member of the extension of P at w in M. (The extension of a variable v at any w, relative to A, is whatever object A assigns to v—it doesn't change from world to world.)

$\ulcorner \sim Q \urcorner$ is true at w in M, relative to A, iff Q is not true at w in M, relative to A. $\ulcorner Q \, \& \, S \urcorner$ is true at w in M, relative to A, iff Q and S are both true at w in M, relative to A. Similar clauses are given for $\ulcorner Q \lor S \urcorner$, $\ulcorner Q \supset S \urcorner$, and $\ulcorner Q \leftrightarrow S \urcorner$.

$\ulcorner \exists v \, Q(v) \urcorner$ is true at w in M, relative to an assignment A, iff there is an object o *in the domain of w* in M such that Q(v) is true at w in M, relative to an assignment A* that assigns o to v and otherwise is just like A. $\ulcorner \forall v \, Q(v) \urcorner$ is true at w in M, relative to A, iff for every object o *in the domain of w* in M, Q(v) is true at w in M, relative to an assignment A* that assigns o to v and otherwise is just like A. (Domain restrictions can be dropped if one wants quantification over all possible individuals.)

$\ulcorner \Box S \urcorner$ is true at w in M, relative to A, iff for all worlds w' such that wRw', S is true at w' in M, relative to A. $\ulcorner \Diamond S \urcorner$ is true at w in M relative to A iff for at least one world w' such that wRw', S is true at w' in M, relative to A.

A sentence S is true at w in M iff S is true at w in M, relative to all assignments. S is *logically true* iff S is true at the "actual world" of every model.

Which sentences are logical truths depends on the restrictions on R, as illustrated by the modal propositional calculus. Without restrictions, the logical truths are those derivable from tautologies plus instances of '$\Box(A \supset B) \supset (\Box A \supset \Box B)$' by *modes ponens* and necessitation (a rule allowing one to prefix '$\Box$' to any theorem). This is system K. Stronger systems, built on K, result from adding restrictions on R. To say that w_2 is possible relative to w_1—$w_1 R w_2$—is to say that if w_1 is, or had been, actual, then w_2 is, or would have been, possible. Since what is actual is surely possible, R is typically required to be reflexive. Two other easily understood, though less obviously justified, constraints are transitivity (if $w_1 R w_2$ and $w_2 R w_3$, then $w_1 R w_3$), and symmetry (if $w_1 R w_2$, then $w_2 R w_1$). Requiring only reflexivity results in system M, which consists of K plus the axiom schema '$\Box A \supset A$.' Adding transitivity results in S4, consisting of M plus '$\Box A \supset \Box\Box A$'. Requiring symmetry (plus reflexivity) instead of transitivity results in B, which consists of M plus '$A \supset \Box\Diamond A$', whereas adding this axiom schema to S4 results in S5, in which R is an equivalence relation—allowing S5 to be simplified by taking every world to be possible relative to every other.[1]

Although S5 is the most popular system, the case for it is vexed. One factor that should have no weight is terminological. If one thinks of the "worlds" in a model as "possible," then some "worlds" posited by K, M, B, and S4 will be *impossible* (relative to the actual world). But surely, one might incautiously think, there can't be any impossible *worlds*. Similarly, if one starts with the idea that members of W are *possible*, then R, which is often called "the accessibility relation," will seem mysterious. If all worlds are possible, what does it mean to say that only some are "accessible"? Without a plausible answer to this question, R may appear to be a mere technical artifact, to be dispensed with in any real logic of necessity; hence S5. However, this reasoning is flawed. The fact that something in a logical model is called a "world" doesn't mean that it is a concrete entity, like our universe, existing in a "pluriverse of alternate realities" (Lewis 2001). It is enough that it be something relative to which sentences and other expressions are evaluated—a maximally complete and informative property that represents the universe as being a certain way—i.e., "a way the world might be."[2]

On this construal, what have been called "worlds" are better called "world-states." The actual world-state is the maximal world-representing property that is instantiated; a possible world-state is one that could have been instantiated. There is no absurdity about impossible world-states, and no mystery about relative possibility. An impossible state isn't something that doesn't, and couldn't have, existed, but a property the universe couldn't have instanti-

---

[1] See Kripke (1963a), (1963b), which also define *truth at world in a model* for quantified systems, and Kripke (1958) for a completeness theorem for the latter. Lewis and Langford (1932) contains an important early discussion.

[2] See Stalnaker (1976) and Soames (2007a).

ated (even if its instantiation is conceivable). As for relative possibility, if there are both possible and impossible world-states, then there will be states w_0, w_1, and w_2 such that w_1 but not w_2 is possible relative to w_0. There is also nothing incoherent in the idea that relative possibility may not be transitive. This will be so if (i) w_0 is actual, and so is instantiated, (ii) w_1 is merely possible, and so could have been instantiated (w_0Rw_1), (iii) had w_1 been instantiated, it would have been the case that w_2 could have been instantiated (w_1Rw_2), even though (iv) since the universe in fact instantiates w_0, w_2 couldn't have been instantiated ($\sim w_0Rw_2$). In a moment, I will illustrate this idea. For now, it is enough not to rule it out.

The question of which modal system to adopt is inseparable from the question of what we want '□' to capture. The number of theoretically significant notions that can usefully be studied from a modal-logical perspective is too large to survey here. However, two contrasting notions are worth special notice. The first is a logico-epistemic concept of necessity according to which $\ulcorner \Box\ S \urcorner$ is true iff S is a logical or analytic truth—that is, a truth the negation of which can't be accepted without inconsistency, or incoherence. The second sense of necessity is metaphysical. In this sense, $\ulcorner \Box\ S \urcorner$ is true iff what S expresses is true and *couldn't have failed to be so, no matter what.* Although standard logical/analytic truths fall into this category, many others do too—e.g., the truth that Saul Kripke is neither David Lewis, nor the square root of 9. Whereas the former notion applies to sentences in virtue of the meanings of their words, the latter applies, in the first instance, to propositions, including some that predicate essential properties of objects. When P expresses an essential property P* of o, $\ulcorner \Box\ (\exists y\ y = x \supset Px) \urcorner$ is true relative to an assignment of o to 'x', because o couldn't have existed without having P*. Since many such *de re* modal claims are true for choices of P which, unlike $\ulcorner (Fx\ v \sim Fx) \urcorner$, are not trivially true of every object, the set of metaphysically necessary truths is larger than the set of logically necessary truths—and their logics are different.

Whereas over a century of formal logic has given us a deep theoretical understanding of logical necessity, our understanding of metaphysical necessity is intuitive—drawn from our ordinary thought and talk about *what would be so if such and such were so and so, what could have been so had certain things been different,* and *what could not be so under any circumstances.* This contrast is connected to another. Although our ordinary thought and talk is permeated with claims about what various individuals could, or could not, do, or be, in various circumstances, there is no established practice, ordinary or theoretical, of calling formulas with free occurrences of variables *logically or analytically true, relative to one assignment of objects, but not another.* In short, *metaphysical* necessity is the province of the modal *de re,* while the logical or conceptual *de re* is all but nonexistent.

As shown in Burgess (1998), there is a historical irony in this. The stated goal of much of the early development of quantified modal systems was to give a logic for *logical* or *analytic necessity.* This was the context into which Quine introduced his infamous arguments against quantifying in. Though his objections were typically overstated—wrongly decrying the unintelligibility of quantification into *any* construction in which substitution of co-extensional terms sometimes fails to preserve truth value—there was a grain of truth in his attack.[3] Noting that *logical truth* and *analyticity* are standardly taken to be properties of sentences, he likened quantification into contexts governed by such operators to the problematic quantification in (1).

1. ∀x 'if x is a cat, x is an animal' is an analytic/logical truth.

Though he didn't put his finger on precisely what is wrong with this, he was right to be dubious. It's not that one can't make quantification into quotes intelligible. One can, as shown in Kaplan (1986). However, the resulting notion of *de re* logical/analytic truth, and accompanying logic, is of little theoretical interest to logicians and mathematicians, and of no interest in capturing any commonsense notion of necessity. The chief philosophical interest in quantified modal logic lies with the metaphysical necessity, essentialism, and nontrivial modal *de re* of Kripke (1972).

With this, we return to S5. Once we have metaphysical necessity, essentialism, and world-states rather than worlds, it is a short

---

[3] In addition to Burgess (1998) and Kaplan (1986), see Quine (1943, 1947, 1953), and Neale (2000b).

step to recognizing metaphysically impossible, but epistemically possible, members of W. These are maximal world-representing properties that couldn't have been instantiated (because they deny that an object has one of its essential properties), but which cannot be known apriori not to be instantiated (Soames 2005a, 2006, 2007a). For example, since nonidentity necessarily relates any pair it actually relates, even though empirical knowledge is needed to determine which pairs these are, world-states in which I am Saul Kripke are epistemically, but not metaphysically, possible.

A related point, involving the essentiality of origin, is made in Salmon (1989). The key example involves a ship s originally constructed from certain material. It is, Salmon plausibly maintains, a necessary truth that if s originated from material m, then s could have originated from material slightly different from m, even though S couldn't have originated from material too different from m (where "too different" is spelled out). Given this, we can construct a series of world-states—beginning with the actual state @ in which S originated from boards $b_1 \ldots b_n$. Each succeeding world-state w_{i+1} substitutes a new board for one of those from which S originated in w_i. Although each state is possible from the preceding one, we are bound to reach world-states that are impossible from @. Thus, relative possibility isn't transitive, and both S4 and S5 fail. Given Salmon's statement of the metaphysical facts, the argument shows that $\ulcorner(\Box P \, \& \sim\Box\Box P)\urcorner$ is true at @, for some P that says that if s exists, then s originated from materials including a certain big enough proportion of the boards $b_1 \ldots b_n$. If this statement is true, it can't be logically false; so neither S4 nor S5 can be the logic of metaphysical necessity. In fact, the conclusion will remain, even if Salmon is wrong about the metaphysical facts, and the statement is false—so long as it is not *logically false,* which it won't be, if, as seems apparent, his story about what is metaphysically possible and what isn't is both conceptually coherent and free of anything that might, independently, be seen to be a *logical* mistake. Thus the argument that neither S4 nor S5 captures the *logic* of necessity is strong.

Semantics, in the sense of a theory of meaning, is, of course, more than a definition of truth in a model, and an accompanying theory of logical truth. To state the truth conditions of sentences one must also specify the intended model, without which the nonlogical vocabulary will remain uninterpreted. For each sentence S, we are after a statement, ⌜For all world-states w, 'S' is true at w iff at w, P⌝, that specifies what the world *must* be like if S is to be true. It is standard in possible worlds semantics to take this 'must' to have the force of metaphysical necessity, and the world-states quantified over to be metaphysically possible. However, if what I have said is correct, this isn't quite right. In addition to metaphysically possible world-states (all of which are also epistemically possible), the intended model must also include epistemically possible, but metaphysically impossible, states. Hence, the semantic theory should tell us, for each S, what it is for S to be true at an arbitrary epistemically possible world-state.

Although these truth conditions are stronger, and more informative, than those provided by Davidson, they aren't enough to establish the theories generating them as theories of meaning. Since sentences true in the same epistemically possible world-states may differ in meaning (consider any two necessary, apriori truths), knowledge even of these strengthened truth conditions is not sufficient for understanding a language. Nor can we identify the meaning of S with the proposition it expresses, if, as is often done in possible worlds semantics, the latter is taken to be the set of world-states at which S is true. It is no small thing to have a theory that specifies the modal truth conditions of sentences; for many philosophical purposes, nothing else is needed. But we still have no justification for taking such a theory to be a theory of meaning.

3.2 ROBERT STALNAKER AND DAVID LEWIS ON COUNTERFACTUALS

One of the most important applications of possible worlds semantics is the account of counterfactual conditionals given in Robert Stalnaker (1968, 1975, 1981a) and David Lewis (1973a). The central problem is of how to understand (2).[4]

---

[4] Although the term 'counterfactual', used to characterize these conditionals, naturally suggests that their antecedents aren't true (at the actual world-state), it is perfectly possible (though perhaps not common) for

2. If it were the case that A, then it would be the case that B. (A $\Box \to$ B)

This problem was illuminatingly discussed in Nelson Goodman (1947, 1955). However, without the machinery of world-states, he was unable to solve it. The basic Stalnaker-Lewis idea is that (2) is true at w iff B is true at world-states w* that differ from w in the minimal amount needed to make A true. If there are world-states possible from w at which A is true (A-states), then (2) is true at w iff some A-states at which B is true are more similar to w than any A-states at which B is false (which, assuming bivalence, means that B is true at all A-states most similar to w); (2) is vacuously true at w if no A-states are possible from w. Stalnaker further assumes, whereas Lewis does not, that in any nonvacuous case in which we evaluate (2), we do so relative to a unique A-state w* selected as more similar to w than any other. Under this assumption, (2) is true at w iff either A is not true at any world-state possible from w, or B is true at w*. Given that either B or its negation will always be true at w*, this assumption leads Stalnaker to embrace the "law" of *Conditional Excluded Middle*—(A $\Box \to$ B) v (A $\Box \to \sim$ B)—which Lewis rejects.

Though this semantic account of counterfactuals is illuminating, one problem stands out. Surely, one is inclined to think, counterfactuals with metaphysically impossible antecedents aren't always true. This is especially evident when the impossibility denies the essence of an individual or a kind—e.g., the impossibility (assuming the essentiality of origin) of Winston Churchill's being my father, or of water's having a molecular structure different

---

true, felicitous uses of them to have true antecedents. For example, a prosecutor might argue, "Ladies and gentlemen, even the defense agrees that *if the defendant had committed the crime, he would have flown into town the night before.* Now we learn that, despite his previous denials, that is precisely what he did—which, when added to the other evidence we have adduced, shows beyond a reasonable doubt that he is, indeed, guilty." A more neutral name for the conditionals represented by (2) is 'subjunctive conditionals'. These contrast with *indicative conditionals*, ⌜If A, then B⌝. The semantic relationship between these conditionals and those of the form (2) is a matter of considerable controversy. See Burgess (2009) for discussion.

from H_2O. For example, the counterfactuals in (3) are naturally taken to be true, while those in (4) are not, despite the fact that the impossible antecedents are the same in the two cases.

    3a. If I (Scott Soames) had been Winston Churchill's son, I would have grown up in England in the first half of the twentieth century.

      b. If water hadn't had the molecular structure H_2O, its freezing and boiling points would have been different (from what they actually are).

    4a. If I (Scott Soames) had been Winston Churchill's son, the United States would have been part of Great Britain.

      b. If water hadn't had the molecular structure H_2O, the history of the Earth would have been no different.

The natural remedy is to expand the analysis to include world-states that are epistemically, but not metaphysically, possible.[5] On this analysis, (2) is true at w iff there are no A-states whatsoever (whether metaphysically possible from w or not), or some A-states at which B is true are more similar to w than any A-states at which B isn't true. The result, given a suitable similarity metric, will be the truth of (3a,b), and the falsity of (4a,b).

But what is similarity? *Not* overall similarity among world-states, as is shown by (5).

    5. If Khrushchev had pushed the button during the Cuban Missile Crisis, there would have been nuclear war.

(5) is true despite the fact that world-states at which the button is pushed and the missiles (miraculously) fail to launch are far more similar overall to the actual world-state than those at which the button is pushed and nuclear war occurs. Examples like these show that the relation labeled "similarity" is really a placeholder for some yet-to-be-articulated relation on world-states that is central to the truth conditions given by the account. The strategy for identifying this relation is to use examples in which the truth

---

[5] I leave it open whether one needs to move to an even less tightly constrained notion of possibility than the notion of epistemic possibility defined here. For discussion, see Nolan (1997).

values of counterfactuals like (5) are clear to eliminate various candidates (e.g., overall similarity) for the target relation, and to support other candidates for the job. Since this identification requires an independent grasp of the conditionals to be analyzed, the Stalnaker-Lewis model does not, itself, constitute an analysis.

The methodology is illustrated by an example in which I have coin-tossing devices A and B, which, when activated, go through a random process that determines whether the coin will land heads or tails. I activate A. While it is running, I offer you a bet on heads, which you decline. The process terminates; the coin is tossed, and lands heads. We now consider (6a,b).

6a. If you had accepted the bet, you would have won.
  b. If I had used device B, the coin would still have landed heads.

Pretheoretically, we judge (6a), but not (6b), to be true. Within the Stalnaker-Lewis framework, this means that, among world-states at which the antecedent of (6a) is true, those "most similar" to the world-state w of the example are ones in which the coin toss has the same outcome as in w. By contrast, among world-states at which that antecedent of (6b) is true, those "most similar" to w contain some at which the coin comes up heads, and others at which it doesn't. Thus, with (6a) sameness of outcome of the toss contributes to the similarity of an antecedent-world to w, while with (6b), it doesn't. Why? The natural thought is that since your decision about the bet has no *causal influence* on whether the coin comes up heads, whereas the device used does, a different decision shouldn't affect the outcome, whereas a different device might. As noted in Kment (2006), this suggests that similarities between two world-states regarding particular matters of fact (e.g., the coin landing heads) contribute to the "similarity" of those states—in the relevant sense—only if these matters of fact have *the same causal history* at both world-states.[6]

Kment goes further, suggesting a natural, though more speculative, extension of this principle, in which '*the same explanation*' is substituted for '*the same causal history*'. Since causal explanation

---

[6] See also Bennett (2003), Edgington (2004), and Schaffer (2004).

is one kind of explanation, the new principle subsumes the old. Since there are also noncausal explanations—as when the fact that one law holds is explained by the holding of another, more fundamental, law—the new principle enlarges the scope of the old. Though this principle falls well short of providing a complete account of similarity, it sharpens our grasp of its extension.

Would such an account of the similarity relation give us an *analysis* of counterfactual conditionals? Not if one requires the *analysans* to be synonymous with the *analysandum*—in the sense in which substitution of one for the other in statements about what one says, means, or thinks always preserves truth. Theories that specify the truth conditions of counterfactual conditionals don't tell us what these sentences mean, or allow us to identify the propositions they express. Philosophical analyses—which are typically nontrivial, highly theoretical, and potentially informative—seldom do. However, such analyses can articulate clear and precise notions capable of playing the roles typically reserved for the *analysandum*. When we have reason to think that a proposed *analysans* A is necessarily equivalent to the *analysandum* B, a demonstration that A applies in a given case can sometimes be used to guide, and even revise, our pretheoretic judgment about B—despite the fact that A doesn't mean the same as B.

In light of this, an *analysis* of counterfactuals along the lines Kment suggests might prove to be possible. However, an important question must be faced, if it does. Is causation to be analyzed in terms of counterfactual dependence, is counterfactual dependence to be analyzed (in part) in terms of causation—or are the two interdependent? This question gains significance from the importance of Lewis's influential analysis of causation. The basic idea, given in Lewis (1973b), is (i) that an event b *causally depends* on a distinct, nonoverlapping event a iff if a were to occur, then b would occur (and if a were not to occur, then b would not occur), and (ii) that an event a^* is *a cause* of a distinct, nonoverlapping event b^* iff b^* is causally dependent on a^*, or there is an event c^* which both causes b^*, and is causally dependent on a^*. So, causation is the ancestral of *causal dependence*.[7]

---

[7] In this analysis Lewis uses so-called "non-backtracking counterfactuals," which hold the past fixed up to the time at which the antecedent is

The thirty-five years since Lewis offered the analysis have seen many objections to, plus qualifications and modifications of, it—the most significant being the revised theory of Lewis (2004). Details aside, however, the direction of the proposed analysis remains the same, with causation being analyzed in terms of counterfactual dependence. This is what is threatened by the suggestion that causation, and/or causal explanation, might be needed for the analysis of the similarity relation in terms of which the truth conditions of counterfactuals are given. On the usual assumption—that analyses express conceptual and explanatory priorities—one or more of these potential analyses can't have that status. Either counterfactuals are not *analyzable* in terms of world-state similarity, or such similarity is not *analyzable* (in part) in terms of the causal features of those states, or causation is not *analyzable* in terms of counterfactual conditionals. Although relations of necessary (and perhaps apriori) equivalence might, in principle, be maintained, mutually exclusive claims of conceptual priority can't be accepted.

Though the resolution of these claims may be philosophically important, it is not required for semantic theories of the meanings and truth conditions of counterfactual conditionals—any more than informative philosophical analyses of knowledge or goodness are needed for semantic theories of sentences containing 'know' or 'good'. Both semantic theories and philosophical analyses may yield claims about truth conditions. However, only those provided by a philosophical analysis are required to be informative in a way that genuinely extends our (nonlinguistic) knowledge. When it comes to meaning, the burden is shifted. Whereas fully adequate semantic theories must (to a first approximation) identify the meanings and propositions expressed by sentences, philosophical analyses of natural-language concepts are not so required.

---

supposed to obtain. This is intended to rule out spurious cases of causal dependence in which b and c are both caused by a, where one might be inclined to reason that if c hadn't occurred, a wouldn't have occurred either, in which case b wouldn't have occurred. In such cases b isn't really causally dependent on c.

A further point relevant to semantic theories of counterfactuals, which has received less attention from those whose goal has been philosophical analysis, is context sensitivity. Some proponents of the Stalnaker-Lewis semantics for counterfactuals have, plausibly, maintained that the standards of similarity used in evaluating them vary from one context to another. The point is illustrated by the contrast between (7a) and (7b).

7a. If Larry Bird's height were the same as mine, he wouldn't have played in the NBA.
  b. If my height were the same as Larry Bird's, we both would have played in the NBA.

Although the consequents of these conditionals are inconsistent with one another, it is easy to imagine conversations in which each is true. In a conversation correctly noting the importance of Larry Bird's height for his greatness in basketball, an utterance of (7a) might plausibly be seen as expressing a truth. In a different conversation correctly noting the effect of my much shorter stature on my athletic career, an utterance of (7b) might (with a some exaggeration of my actual ability) be seen as true. If we further suppose (i) that any world-state at which 'A's height is the same as B's' is true is a world-state at which 'B's height is the same as A's' is also true, and (ii) that because of this the class of world-states at which the antecedent of (7a) is true is the same as the class of world-states at which the antecedent of (7b) is true, then the different truth values of the two sentences, as used in their respective contexts, may naturally be attributed, on the Stalnaker-Lewis semantics, to the incorporation of different presupposed standards of similarity into the propositions expressed in those contexts. In the former context, world-states in which I maintain my actual height, and Larry Bird's decreases to match it, count as more similar to the actual world-state than do world-states in which Bird maintains his actual height, and mine increases to match it (or both change to some third height). In the latter context, the relative similarity metric is reversed. Whereas those concerned with philosophical analysis often follow Lewis in focusing on what they regard as a "default" setting for the similarity relation, those whose aim is more specifically linguistic need to inquire more closely into the ways in which contexts contribute to the propositions expressed (or asserted) by (utterances of) counterfactual conditionals.

3.3 THE MONTAGOVIAN VISION

The small sample of possible worlds semantics touched on so far illustrates a research program in philosophical logic of great significance for the philosophy of language. Starting with the predicate calculus, one enriches the system piece by piece, adding operators and constructions incorporating philosophically significant features of natural language. So far we have looked at modal operators and counterfactual conditionals. In the next chapter, we will add temporal ("tense") operators, indexicals, and demonstratives. Though certain additions to classical logic, e.g., temporal operators and counterfactuals, have some relevance to formalizations of science, broadly conceived, other additions have very little, and none advance the original goal of formalizing mathematics. Modality is, of course, central to philosophy, and it is a great boon to have both a formal language for clearly and unambiguously expressing modal claims, and a rigorous, well-understood formal system for reasoning with, and about, them. Since the subject matter of philosophy is essentially unrestricted, similar, though more limited, points can be made about the potential significance of other additions to the languages of classical logic.

The value of these systems is not limited to the uses to which they can be put. Equally important is their role as prototypes of well-understood languages in which precise truth-theoretic semantic rules function in parallel with explicitly formulated syntactic rules. As the research program advances, and more and more features of natural language are formally represented, the languages of which we have good truth-theoretic grasp become more complex, powerful, and natural-language like. Extending results so far achieved, one can imagine a time at which enriched descendants of the original classical languages approach, or even match, the full expressive power of natural language, giving us a kind of understanding of English, *by proxy*.

This is one strategy for understanding natural language that emerges from the tradition in philosophical logic stretching from Frege's *Begriffsschrift* to Kripke's modal semantics. At that point, however, a more radical strategy emerged from the work of Richard Montague.[8] Instead of starting with classical systems, adding formal counterparts of central features of natural language, and using the resulting formulas to "regiment" English sentences (prescriptive), or pose as their "logical forms" (putatively descriptive), Montague specifies syntactic rules that generate English, or English-like, structures directly, while pairing each such rule with a truth-theoretic rule interpreting it. This close parallel between syntax and semantics is what makes the languages of classical logic so transparently tractable, and what they were designed to embody. Montague's bold contention is that we don't have to replace natural languages with formal substitutes to achieve such transparency, because the same techniques employed to *create* formal languages can be used to *describe* natural languages in mathematically revealing ways.[9]

---

[8] See in particular Montague (1970, 1973), and the introduction of Thomason (1974), all in Thomason (1974).

[9] There is one ironic caveat worth noting at the outset. Although standard Tarski-style semantic theories for familiar formal languages typically pair each syntactic rule with a semantic rule interpreting the expressions that result from it, these systems are not compositional in Montague's strict sense—because the extension of $\ulcorner \forall v\ (P) \urcorner$ *relative to an assignment A of values to variables* is not a function of the extension (or intension) of P *relative to A*. See Salmon (2006). Since Montague requires the semantic rule interpreting the output of a syntactic rule R to specify the extension of the complex expression generated by R from the extensions or intensions of its parts, the usual Tarski rules for quantification don't fit. This doesn't mean that compositional semantic theories can't be given for these languages. With some inelegant fussing, one can specify the extensions of compound expressions, *unrelativized to assignments,* as functions of the unrelativized extensions of their parts. The important point, however, is that there is no need to do this. The non-compositionality of typical Tarski-style semantics in no way diminishes the tractability of these formal languages, or obscures the transparency of the relationship between their syntax and semantics. The lesson here reinforces an

The idea is illustrated by simple examples, starting with (8a), which would standardly be regimented in the propositional calculus by (8b).

8a. Every man snores.
  b. $\forall x$ (Man x $\supset$ Snores x)

Whereas (8b) is multiclausal, containing terms 'Man' and 'Snores' of the same grammatical category, plus a simple, unrestricted quantifier, (8a) is monoclausal, containing the common noun 'man' and the intransitive verb 'snores', the first of which is a constituent of a complex quantifier phrase. Montagovian analyses of (8a) should reflect these facts. On one such analysis, 'every' is a determiner, which combines with the common noun 'man' to form the noun phrase 'every man', from which (8a) is constructed by substituting that phrase for the pronoun/variable 'he$_1$' in the formula 'he$_1$ snores'—gotten by combining 'he$_1$' with 'snores'. Corresponding to these three syntactic rules are three semantic rules interpreting them. Rule 1 tells us that the extension of 'he$_1$ snores' = the extension of 'snores' = the set of snorers. Rule 2, interpreting the noun phrase, assigns the set of all sets containing every man as extension, given, as input, the set of men (the extension of 'man'), and the function that assigns to any set s the set of all sets that contain every member of s (the extension of 'every'). Rule 3, interpreting (8a), assigns it truth iff the extension of 'he$_1$ snores' is in the extension of the noun phrase.

Next consider (9a), which is ambiguous between readings represented in the predicate calculus by (9b) and (9c).

9a. Every man loves some woman.
  b. $\forall x$ (Man x $\supset$ $\exists y$ (Woman y & Loves x,y))
  c. $\exists y$ (Woman y & $\forall x$ (Man x $\supset$ Loves x, y))

---

important point I will make below about Montague's treatment of English and other natural languages. While his strategy of treating them on their own terms—without regimentation into classical systems of logic—is salutary, his rigid insistence on a one-to-one isomorphism between syntactic and strictly compositional semantic rules goes beyond what is required in order to achieve a clear, illuminating, and scientific understanding of both formal and natural languages.

For Montague, the ambiguity is captured by different syntactic derivations of (9a) from the formula 'he$_1$ loves her$_1$', the extension of which is the set of pairs the first of which loves the second. The reading corresponding to (9b) arises from a derivation in which 'some woman' is substituted for the pronoun/variable 'her$_1$', producing 'he$_1$ loves some woman'. Rule 2 above gives the set of all sets containing some woman as the extension of 'some woman'—determined from the set of women, and the function that assigns to any set s the set of all sets that contain a member of s. Rule 3 then gives us the extension of 'he$_1$ loves some woman', which is the set of individuals i such that the set of individuals j loved by i is in the extension of 'some woman'. Since this is the set of individuals who love at least one woman, the final application of Rule 3—interpreting the substitution of 'every man' for 'he$_1$' in 'he$_1$ loves some woman'—tells us that, on this syntactic analysis, (9a) is true iff the set of those who love at least one woman contains every man. To get the reading corresponding to (9c), we reverse the order of construction, substituting 'every man' for 'he$_1$' in 'he$_1$ loves her$_1$', to get 'every man loves her$_1$'—the extension of which is the set of individuals j such that the set of individuals i who love j contains every man. So, when (9a) is derived by substituting 'some woman' for 'her$_1$', it is true iff the set of those loved by every man includes at least one woman.[10]

Examples (10–11) illustrate variable binding, and the treatment of intensionality.

10a. *Every man* believes that some woman loves *him*.
  b. she$_1$ loves him$_1$
  c. 'some woman' + (b) $\Rightarrow$ 'some woman loves him$_1$'
  d. 'that' + (c) $\Rightarrow$ 'that some woman loves him$_1$'
  e. he$_1$ believes that some woman loves him$_1$
  f. every man + (e) $\Rightarrow$ (10a)
  11. *John* believes that some woman loves *him*.

---

[10] For Montague, the different readings of the sentence are assigned to different *syntactic analyses* of the sentence, which are given by the different *derivations* of the sentence.

Starting with (10b), we introduce the quantified noun phrase, as before, giving us a formula the extension of which is the set of individuals loved by at least one woman. The intensional operator 'that' combines with this formula, yielding its intension (the function from world-states w to sets of individuals loved by at least one woman at w) as the extension of the 'that'-clause. Formula (e) is gotten by combining (10d) with the transitive verb 'believes', applying to pairs of individuals and propositions, represented as functions from world-states to truth values.[11] The extension of (10e) is, then, the set of individuals i such that i bears the belief relation to the extension of (10d) relative to an assignment of i to 'he$_1$'/'him$_1$' (which is a function from world-states to truth values). Moving to (10f) we get the result that, on this syntactic analysis, (10a) is true iff the set of individuals who believe themselves to be loved by at least one woman contains every man.

The anaphoric relationship between pronoun and antecedent in (11) was one of Montague's reasons for treating proper names as members of the same syntactic/semantic category as quantifier phrases. Since 'John' and 'every man' are both Montagovian "term phrases," (11) has a derivation just like (10a). Taking the extension of 'John' to be the set of all sets containing its bearer, the theory correctly predicts that (11) is true iff the set of individuals who believe themselves to be loved by at least one woman includes John.

Though startling, this assimilation of names to quantifiers has additional Montagovian benefits. Both are traditionally counted as noun phrases in English grammar, and both can be subjects of sentences, as well as objects of transitive verbs and prepositions. For Montague, verb phrases combine with terms (including names and quantifier phrases) to form sentences. Since there is a single such rule for forming such sentences, there must be a single rule interpreting them. Since verb phrases denote sets,

---

[11] Whereas Montague (1973) collapses (d) and (e) into one step by treating 'believe that' as a kind of intensional transitive verb that combines with a sentence to form a verb phrase, breaking 'that' out as a separate syntactic and semantic unit is more revealing, and captures more cases— e.g., 'Joe believes the proposition Bob asserted'.

and quantifiers denote sets of sets, a subject-predicate sentence of this sort is true iff the verb phrase extension is in the extension of the subject. When one switches the subject from 'every man' to 'John', this requires 'John' to denote the set of all sets containing its bearer. Analogous points apply to the rules interpreting transitive verbs and prepositions. Since both take names and quantifier phrases as objects, uniform interpretations of the resulting phrases require a uniform analysis of names and quantifiers.

The point is illustrated by (12a) and (12b), both of which are ambiguous, with one reading requiring the quantifier phrase to combine with a transitive verb, or preposition, to form a phrase, preceding the construction of the formula, and another reading in which the formula is initially constructed using a pronoun/variable, for which the quantifier phrase is then substituted, in the manner of previous examples.

12a. John seeks a unicorn.
  b. John talks about a unicorn.

In derivation 1 of (12a), the transitive verb 'seeks' combines with the term 'a unicorn' to form the verb phrase 'seeks a unicorn', which then combines with the subject 'John' to form the sentence. 'Seeks' is intensional—which is to say that its extension maps the *intension* of its object-argument, 'a unicorn', onto the extension of the resulting verb phrase. The intension of 'a unicorn' is a function from possible world-states w to the set of all sets containing at least one unicorn at w, and the extension of the verb phrase is the set of individuals who bear the seeking relation to this intension. Since it is possible for an individual to bear that relation to this intension (to try, in effect, to find an instantiator of unicornhood), without there actually being any unicorns, (12a) can be true, even though there are no unicorns. Analogous remarks apply to a parallel derivation of (12b). By contrast, (12a) has another derivation in which it arises from the formula 'John seeks him_1' by substituting 'a unicorn' for the pronoun/variable, by the same rule used in earlier examples. Since the extension of the formula is the set of individuals sought by John, (12a) is true, on this syntactic analysis, iff that set is a member of the set of sets containing at least one unicorn—iff at least one x is both a unicorn and sought by John. On this analysis, the truth of (12a), like that of a corresponding analysis of (12b), requires the existence of unicorns.[12]

These examples support admitting quantifier phrases into the same category as names, so that they can combine with intensional transitive verbs like 'seek' and intensional prepositions like 'about'. Examples (10) and (11) support admitting names into the same category as quantifier phrases, to achieve a unified account of variable binding. The similarity of names and quantifier phrases with respect to many syntactic processes of phrase and

---

[12] In Montague (1973), the semantic system is set up so that (i) the extension of a verb phrase is a set of individual concepts (i.e., a set of functions from world-states to individuals) rather than a set of individuals, (ii) the extension of a term is a property of properties of individual concepts, rather than a set of sets of individuals, and (iii) a sentence gotten from combining a verb phrase VP with a subject term T is true iff the intension of VP (a property of individual concepts) has the property denoted by T (which will hold iff the intension of VP is in the set of properties determined by the denotation of T). Meaning postulates are then used to reinstate extensionality when recourse to the intensional isn't needed. For example, there is a meaning postulate ensuring that in all but a few specially marked cases, the official truth condition for a sentence formed from T and VP is equivalent to one that requires the set of *individuals* (determined by the individual concepts in the official extension of VP) to be in the set of sets determined by the official extension of T. In such cases, I speak informally of the extensions of VP and T *as if* they were a set of individuals, and a set of sets of individuals, respectively. A different meaning postulate guarantees that verb phrases formed from combining ordinary, non-intensional transitive verbs (like 'find' or 'eat', but unlike 'seek') with terms are extensional in their object position, while still another meaning postulate establishes extensionality for prepositional phrases headed by, e.g., 'in', but not 'about'. In the second derivation of (12a), the rule combining 'John seeks him$_1$' with the quantifier phrase officially treats the quantification as ranging over functions from world-states to individuals. However, another meaning postulate governing ordinary common nouns, including 'unicorn', guarantees that the functions will be constant—rigidly returning the same object as value for each world-state as argument. The effect of this is to render the quantification over individuals. Thus, on this reading (12a) is true only if there exists at least one unicorn and John is looking for that very unicorn.

sentence construction lead, in the presence of Montague's insistence on a strict isomorphism between syntactic and semantic rules, to treating them as taking semantic values of the same type. Such is Montague's case for assimilating names to quantifiers.

However, doubts remain. How likely is it that language users should have introduced words and phrases expressing properties, and quantifier phrases expressing higher-order properties, without first having words designating individuals to which ordinary properties are attributed? And if proper names aren't such words, what are? Like names and quantifier phrases, demonstratives—'he', 'she', 'it', 'this', and 'that'—can (i) combine with prepositions, transitive verbs, and verb phrases to form propositional phrases, verb phrases, and sentences, and (ii) serve as antecedents of anaphoric pronouns of the kind illustrated by (10) and (11). Are they also to be treated as quantifiers? As a formal matter, they could be, though it is hard to imagine them being so understood by ordinary speakers. To make matters worse, suppose we were now to introduce a new set of terms by explicitly stipulating that they were to be genuine names and demonstratives, used to designate individuals. Surely, it's not beyond our power to do that. Nor is it beyond our power to use these new terms in sentences as subjects, as well as objects of verbs and prepositions. It would be very surprising if they couldn't also serve as antecedents of anaphoric pronouns. But if all of this is possible, without the terms being quantifiers, then the quantificational analysis of ordinary names is doubtful.

The issues raised by this discussion have implications both for Montague's overall theoretical perspective, and for the syntactic and semantic analyses of various particular constructions. At the most general level, it is, I think, hard to overestimate the value of his central insight: there is no need to force one's account of the semantic structure of natural language into the Procrustean bed of classical logic, which was initially developed to avoid the complexities of natural language. His account of quantifier phrases in natural language was both seminal and liberating. The same is true of his treatment of many grammatical types not found in classical logical languages, including verb-phrase-modifying adverbs ('slowly', 'allegedly', 'nearly'), common-noun-modifying adjectives ('alleged', 'former', 'heavy', 'American'), adjective-forming prepositions ('in', 'of'), adverb-forming prepositions ('with', 'of', 'about'), intensional transitive verbs ('seek', 'worship', 'conceive'), and verb-phrase-taking verbs ('try to', 'want to').[13] Both his own work, and that of those who have followed him, have done much to bring such expressions within the scope of formal semantics.

However, Montague's insistence on maintaining the logician's one-to-one correspondence between syntactic and compositional semantic rules when investigating natural language was itself an apriori commitment lacking empirical justification. One sees what was, perhaps, a tacit recognition of this in his reliance on meaning postulates—restricting acceptable interpretations of his English-like fragments to those validating them. Since these often have the effect of treating different members of the same syntactic/semantic category differently, they undermine the desired isomorphism that is so central to the program. Since Montague didn't articulate any general criterion for when appeal to meaning postulates is justified and when it isn't, he must, at some level, have recognized the futility of trying to determine, in advance, how close the syntax and semantics of natural languages will turn out to be. It is heartening, therefore, that later work has followed an empirically balanced approach that includes many of his innovative semantic techniques, while giving empirically motivated theories of English syntax their due.[14]

With this in mind, let us return to the factors that led to the quantificational analysis of names. As we have seen, the strict isomorphism between syntax and semantic motivating the analysis won't bear the weight placed on it. In the case of variable binding, there are natural ways of accounting for the similarity of the anaphora in (10a) and (11), without taking names to be

[13] Montague's framework also provides the basis for a richer account of sentence adverbs. Though he doesn't say much about how to distinguish them from verb-phrase-modifying adverbs, this is usefully discussed in Stalnaker and Thomason (1973).

[14] See Dowty, Wall, and Peters (1981) and Partee (2004).

quantifiers.[15] Even the ingenious analysis of (12a,b) in which their truth does not require the existence of unicorns suffers from serious limitations inherent in Montague's framework. Consider, for example, the analogous cases (13a,b).

13a. John seeks *a solution to the decision problem for first-order logic.*
  b. John talks about *a solution to the decision problem for first-order logic.*

Reasoning as we did in (12), we may take the intension of the quantified phrase 'a solution to the decision problem for first-order logic' to be the function from possible world-states w to the set of all sets containing at least one solution to the decision problem for first-order logic at w. Since it is a necessary, and apriori, truth that the decision problem for first-order validity is unsolvable, this function returns the empty set as value for every world-state as argument. It is doubtful that we can make sense of this degenerate intension as the object of John's search—and even if we could, the system would give us the incorrect result that (13a,b) and (14a,b) have the same truth value for every NP with the same degenerate intension as the quantified phrase in (13a,b).

14a. John seeks *NP.*
  b. John talks about *NP.*

On certain natural assumptions, a version of this problem afflicts (12a,b) themselves. If 'unicorn' is a natural kind term that fails to designate any natural kind, then it is analogous to a proper name, or occurrence of a demonstrative, that fails to denote. As we will see in chapter 4, there are reasons to think that each such term rigidly designates the same thing at all possible world-states. So, if 'unicorn' fails to denote at the actual world-state, it will fail to denote at every state. Given this, we get the same problem for

---

[15] Soames (1994a) includes both such an alternative, and an argument (on pp. 257–58) that there are instances of the kind of binding illustrated in (10) and (11) that can't be handled by making the antecedent a quantifier, because, in these cases, the antecedent is itself a pronoun functioning as a variable bound by an earlier quantifier.

(12) that we got for (13). Since the analysis of (12) was one of the notable innovations of Montague (1973), this may be a serious defect.

This defect is related to a larger structural problem: the inability of systems of *intensional* semantics—in which sentences are evaluated at possible world-states and/or moments of time, and semantic rules assign extensions and intensions to expressions on the basis of those of their parts—to account for *intentional* phenomena. The most obvious of these are propositional attitudes—assertion, denial, belief, doubt, etc.—and the attitude ascriptions that express them. Since the problems posed by these constructions, and the needed solutions, will be addressed later, we need not go into greater detail now. The crucial point about intensional transitive verbs is that since they are of a piece with other *intentional* constructions, the resources required for an adequate treatment of them are not available in Montague's system.[16]

The framework suffers from other systemic problems. Like all strictly truth-conditional semantic theories, none of its theorems identify the meanings of sentences, and knowledge of the whole set of theorems doesn't suffice for understanding the language. One can extract a set of possible world-states (and times) to be called "propositions" from a definition of truth at a world-state (and time) *in the intended model*. However, since sentences can differ in meaning despite being true at the same world-states (and times), such propositions can't be the meanings of sentences. Similarly, even if the theory provides true, informative theorems ⌜For all world-states w (and times t) 'S' is true at w (and t) iff at w (and t), P⌝, knowing them will always be compatible with misunderstanding the sentences, and believing falsehoods about what they mean. For these reasons, no strictly truth-conditional theory of the sort envisioned by Montague will ever qualify as a genuine theory of meaning.

---

[16] Apparently non-denoting natural kind terms like 'unicorn', as well as apparently non-denoting proper names, pose special problems, even for theories of 'structured propositions' capable of accommodating (13)—if, as Kripke argues, the meanings of names and natural kind terms are not Fregean senses. Salmon (1998) proposes a solution.

Nevertheless, it could be quite valuable. It would be useful to have a theory that generated correct and informative claims about the semantic structure of English, and the (modal) truth conditions of its sentences, even if it fell short of being a theory of meaning. For many purposes, it might be all we need. However, it is not clear that even the best Montagovian semantic theory will take us that far. The difficulty is not with the recursive definition of truth *in a model*, or with the account of significant semantic structure. Rather, it lies with specifying the *intended model* in such a way that, when combined with the truth definition, it allows us to derive correct, informative, instances of (15).

15. For all world-states w (and times t) 'S' is true at w (and t) iff at w (and t), P.

Think of the rules for assigning extensions to phrases like 'alleged murderer' from the extension of the adjective 'alleged' and the intension of the common noun 'murderer'. The latter can be taken to be a function m from world-states to sets of individuals that have murdered at those states. The former will be a function f that maps the intension of its argument onto the extension of the resulting phrase. Which function is it? I am not here asking for a definition of 'alleged', simply a specification of f that can be used in deriving statements like (16).

16. 'The man in the corner is an alleged murderer' is true at w iff at w the man in the corner is an alleged murderer.

We know that, at w, f must map m onto the set of individuals alleged to be murderers at w. Similarly for other arguments of f. How are we to generalize this into a specification we can use? Since there are infinitely possible arguments f can take, we can't simply list one clause for each case. Can we say that *f maps any such argument g to the set of individuals i alleged, at w, to be members of g(w)*? Not if this means (a) *that g(w) is such that i is alleged to be a member of it*, since one can be alleged to be a member of the set containing Bill and Mary (who are all and only the murderers in w), without being alleged, at w, to be a murderer; and also not if it means (b) *that allegations about i mention g or w*, since one can be an alleged murderer at w without any allegation having been made about g or w.[17] Similar worries can be raised about the treatment of 'fake', 'artificial', and 'toy'.

Clearly, there is a problem here in generating elementary statements of truth conditions like (16). Whether or not it is simply another instance of the long reach of the *intentional* remains to be seen. Since 'alleged' is intentional, it is sensitive to *hyper-intensional* differences in its arguments. Something can be an alleged formalization of second-order logic without being an alleged *incomplete* formalization of second-order logic, even though it is a necessary, apriori truth that all formalizations of second-order logic are incomplete. This suggests that the problem in the previous paragraph can't be solved for 'alleged' in Montague's framework, and hence that the theory won't provide us with correct, and only correct, statements of truth conditions, along the lines of (16). Whether or not this problem extends to any non-intentional cases is less clear. What does seem clear is that despite the indisputable fruitfulness of Montague's illuminating innovations in formal semantics, there are serious limitations to the positive results obtainable within the framework he created.

Selected Further Reading

Burgess, John (1998), "Quinus ab omni naevo vindicatus."
——— (1999), "Which Modal Logic Is the Right One?"
Heim, Irene (1982), *The Semantics of Definite and Indefinite Noun Phrases.*
Kamp, Hans (1981), "A Theory of Truth and Semantic Representation."

---

[17] Following strategy (b) we could derive *'The man in the corner is an alleged murderer' is true at w iff, at w, the man in the corner is alleged to be a member of the set of individuals that is the value of the function g—which assigns to any possible world-state the set of murderers at that state—at the argument w.* However, this is only an approximation of what we want. Although this statement of truth conditions might literally be true if all speakers of English were conscious Montague semanticists, who routinely employ the abstract machinery of intensional logic, it is not true in the language of ordinary speakers.

———— (1995), Discourse Representation Theory."

Lewis, David (1973a), *Counterfactuals*.

Montague, Richard (1973), "The Proper Treatment of Quantification in Ordinary English."

Partee (2004), *Compositionality in Formal Semantics: Selected Papers*.

Salmon, Nathan (1989), "On the Logic of What Might Have Been."

Stalnaker, Robert (1984), *Inquiry*.

Thomason, Richmond (1974), ed., *Formal Philosophy: Selected Papers of Richard Montague*, Introduction.

Rigid Designation, Direct Reference, and Indexicality

4.1 BACKGROUND

The contributions of Saul Kripke and David Kaplan discussed in this chapter are leading elements of a body of work that changed the course of analytic philosophy. Prior to it, T1–T5 were widely accepted; afterwards they were not.

T1. The meaning of a term is never its referent, but rather is a descriptive sense that provides necessary and sufficient conditions for determining reference.

T2. Since the meaning of a word, as used by a speaker s, is the sense s mentally associates with it, if two words have the same meaning and s understands both, then s should be able to recognize that they do. In addition to being transparent, meanings and mental contents are determined by factors internal to speakers.

T3. The apriori, the necessary, and the analytic are one and the same.

T4. Claims about objects having or lacking properties essentially, independently of how they are described, make no sense. Even if t designates o and ⌜Necessarily t is F, if t exists⌝ is true, there will always be another term t* designating o for which ⌜Necessarily t* is F, if t* exists⌝ is false. Since it would be arbitrary to give either sentence priority in determining the essential properties of o, the idea that o has, or lacks, such properties must be relativized to how o is described.

T5. Since the job of philosophy is not to discover contingent, aposteriori truths, its task is conceptual clarification, which proceeds by the analysis of meaning.

4.2 KRIPKE ON NAMES, NATURAL KIND TERMS, AND NECESSITY

4.21 *Rigid Designation, Essentialism, and Nonlinguistic Necessity*

The necessity featured in *Naming and Necessity* is the nonlinguistic notion needed for quantified modal logic and the modal *de re*.[1] Kripke's articulation of this notion is linked to his discussion of *rigid designation,* and *metaphysical essentialism.* According to his technical definition, t rigidly designates o iff t designates o at every world-state at which o exists, and never designates anything else. The import of this definition may be illustrated using the name 'Aristotle', which rigidly designates a certain man m. Since 'Aristotle liked dogs' is true at w iff the referent of 'Aristotle' at w liked dogs at w, the sentence is true at w iff m liked dogs at w. In other words, what we (here and now) use 'Aristotle liked dogs' to express is something that would have been true had the world been in state w iff the man we, here and now, use 'Aristotle' to refer to, would have liked dogs had the world been in state w.[2] This result matches what we, pretheoretically, take to be obvious: the truth or falsity of the sentence, as used by us to describe any counterfactual situation, depends only on Aristotle's attitudes toward dogs in that situation.

For Kripke, an essential property is one an object could not exist without having; an accidental property is one it could have lacked. Being a philosopher, a father, and an American are among my accidental properties; being human, being made up of molecules, and not being identical with Saul Kripke are good candi-

---

[1] Kripke (1972). Citations will be to the 1980 version.

[2] Although the world-states in Kripke's definition are metaphysically possible, the definition can be broadened to include epistemically possible, but metaphysically impossible, states. When this is done ordinary names remain rigid, although some definite descriptions that satisfy the definition when world-states are required to be metaphysically possible cease to do so. A further extension of Kripke—according to which ordinary proper names designate their referents even at world-states at which those referents don't exist—will also be assumed here.

dates for being essential properties. The connection between rigid designation and essentiality is expressed by (1).

1. If t is a rigid designator of o, and F expresses P, then the claim that P is an essential property of o is equivalent to the claim ⌜it is necessary that if t exists, then t is F⌝.

This connection gives the lie to Quine's influential objection, T4, to essentialism. Since a rigid designator t of o picks out o at all world-states at which o exists, the question of whether o has P essentially—i.e., at all metaphysically possible world-states at which o exists—is equivalent to the question of whether ⌜it is necessary that if t exists, then t is F⌝ is true (where F expresses P). Since the truth values of other sentences containing *nonrigid* terms are irrelevant, T4 collapses.[3]

With rigid designation and nontrivial essentialism comes the demise of T3. Assuming that being human, being made up of molecules, and being nonidentical with Kripke are essential properties of anything that has them, we must recognize (2a,b) as being true at all metaphysically possible world-states, and hence as being necessary, if they are true at all.

2a. Scott Soames is a human being, if Scott Soames exists.
 b. Scott Soames is made up of molecules, if Scott Soames exists.
 c. Scott Soames ≠ Saul Kripke.

However, knowledge of these truths can only be had by appeal to empirical evidence, so they are not apriori. Since the required evidence is not needed merely to understand the sentences, they are also not analytic. Because there are nonanalytic, necessary,

---

[3] Kripke's rebuttal doesn't *prove* the intelligibility or correctness of nontrivial essentialism; it *reinstates* the pretheoretic intelligibility and plausibility of the doctrine, by removing a fallacious objection. In so doing it transfers the burden of proof back to the skeptic to show that our ordinary essentialist thought and talk are incoherent, or unsupported. The dialectical situation involving Quine's objection, Kripke's rebuttal, the Quinean reply, and a further Kripkean rebuttal is discussed on pp. 347–54 of Soames (2003b).

aposteriori truths, T3 fails. T5, which confines philosophy to the analysis of meaning, presupposes T3, and so is also threatened.

The modal *de re*, expressed by quantifying in, follows unproblematically. Like names, variables are rigid. The referent of 'x' relative to an assignment A is whatever A assigns as referent of 'x' (no matter what the world-state). $\ulcorner\exists x \ \Box \ Fx\urcorner$ is true at @ iff for some o, $\ulcorner\Box \ Fx\urcorner$ is true relative to an assignment A of o to 'x', which, in turn, is true iff Fx is true relative to A, at all world-states possible from @—i.e., iff at every such state, o has that property expressed by F. Given this, plus our previous results about (2a,b,c), we can establish (3a,b,c).

3a. ∃x (x is a human being, and it couldn't have been the case that x existed without being a human being)

b. ∃x (x is made up of molecules, and it couldn't have been the case that x existed without being made up of molecules)

c. ∃x (necessarily x ≠ Saul Kripke)

4.22 *The Nondescriptive Semantics of Names*

Kripke argues against two versions of descriptivism.

Strong Version: Descriptions associated with names by speakers *give the meanings* (semantic contents) of names and determine their referents at world-states.

<u>Corollary 1</u>: Since the meaning of n is the same as that of D, the referent of n at w is the denotation of D at w, which is whatever uniquely satisfies D at w; thus $\ulcorner$n is F$\urcorner$ is true at w iff $\ulcorner$D is F$\urcorner$ is true at w, and $\ulcorner$if n exists, then n is D$\urcorner$ is true at all possible world-states, and so is a necessary truth. *Substitution of D for n preserves the modal profile.*

<u>Corollary 2</u>: Since the meaning of n is given by D, $\ulcorner$n is F$\urcorner$ and $\ulcorner$D is F$\urcorner$ express the same proposition, as do $\ulcorner$if n exists, then n is D$\urcorner$ and $\ulcorner$if D exists, then D is D$\urcorner$. So, anyone who believes/knows the proposition expressed by one believes/knows the proposition expressed by the other. *Substitution of D for n preserves the epistemic profile.*

>   *Weak Version*: Descriptions associated with a name n by speak-
>   ers semantically *fix the referent of n* at the actual world-
>   state, without giving its meaning. Once reference is fixed, n
>   is stipulated to retain that referent at other world-states.
>
>   <u>Corollaries</u>: (i) The speaker s associates a description D with n
>   that s takes to be uniquely satisfied. (ii) o is the referent of n
>   iff o uniquely satisfies D. (iii) Since s knows this on the basis
>   of s's semantic knowledge, s knows on the basis of semantic
>   knowledge alone that if ⌜n exists⌝ expresses a truth, ⌜n is D⌝
>   does too.

Kripke's *modal argument* targets Corollary 1 of the strong version
of descriptivism. Since names are rigid designators, whereas the
descriptions standardly associated with them by speakers are not,
these descriptions don't give the meanings of the names. An intuitive test that classifies 'Aristotle' as rigid, while classifying 'the
greatest student of Plato', 'the founder of formal logic', and any
other descriptions of Aristotle in terms of his achievements as
nonrigid, is given by R.[4]

>   R. A term t is rigid iff ⌜the individual who is/was t could not
>   have existed without being t, and no one other than t could
>   have been t⌝ expresses a truth; otherwise t is nonrigid.

Since substitution of any such nonrigid description for 'Aristotle'
fails to preserve the modal profiles of some sentences, the strong
version of descriptivism is falsified.

Kripke's argument assumes that the descriptions standardly
associated with names by speakers are nonrigid. However, this
assumption can be challenged. Consider the operator 'actually',
which, when added to ⌜the x: Fx⌝, produces a description ⌜the x:
actually Fx⌝ that, when used at the actual world-state @, designates an object o at any world-state w iff o is the only object
at w that satisfies F at @. With this operator, the proponent of
strong descriptivism can rigidify any description that designates a

---

[4] Although descriptions are most naturally thought of as generalized
quantifiers, irrelevant complications can be avoided by treating them
here as complex singular terms.

unique object at @, thereby attempting to circumvent the modal argument. However, since substitution of such a description for a name often changes *the epistemic profile* of a sentence, the attempt can't succeed, as is shown by the truth of (4).

4. It is possible to believe that Aristotle is $\mathscr{G}$ without believing that the x: actually $\mathscr{F}$x is $\mathscr{G}$.

As used at @, (4) is true iff for some possible agent A and world-state w, A believes, at w, that Aristotle is $\mathscr{G}$ without believing, at w, that *the thing that is $\mathscr{F}$at @* is $\mathscr{G}$—i.e., without believing, *of @*, that the individual who is $\mathscr{F}$*there* is $\mathscr{G}$ (at w). Since believing, at w, that Aristotle is $\mathscr{G}$ doesn't require having beliefs about @, (4) is true. Since the argument can be given for any name and 'actually'-rigidified description, no such description gives the meaning of any name.[5]

The case is strengthened by an independent refutation of Corollary 2.

(i) Let D be either a nonrigid, or an 'actually'-rigidified, description. If D gave the meaning of n, then $\ulcorner$n is F$\urcorner$ would express the same proposition as $\ulcorner$D is F$\urcorner$. So anyone who knew or believed one would know or believe the other, and $\ulcorner$Ralph knows/believes that n is F$\urcorner$ and $\ulcorner$Ralph knows/believes that D is F$\urcorner$ would agree in truth value. Since $\ulcorner$if n exists, then n is D$\urcorner$ would express the same proposition as $\ulcorner$if D exists, then D is D$\urcorner$, it would be knowable apriori, and $\ulcorner$it is knowable apriori that if n exists, then n is D$\urcorner$ would be true.

(ii) When D is a description concerning the well-known achievements or characteristics of the referent of an ordinary name n, the conditions in (i) are not satisfied.

(iii) So, D doesn't give the meaning of n.

Our knowledge that Aristotle was a philosopher, logician, and student of Plato rests on empirical evidence. If, for some reason, that evidence were found to be questionable, and further inde-

---

[5] See Soames (2002), 39–50. Here, and throughout, '$\mathscr{F}$' and '$\mathscr{G}$' are schematic letters.

pendent evidence were not available, we would have no way of knowing these things. So, if D involves such characteristics, and p is expressed by ⌜Aristotle was D⌝, our knowledge of p is aposteriori, and ⌜it is knowable apriori that if Aristotle existed, then Aristotle was D⌝ is false. Hence D doesn't give the meaning of 'Aristotle'.

Having disposed of strong descriptivism, Kripke turns to the weak version, noting that if D merely fixes n's referent, then n will be rigid even when D is not. In such cases, ⌜n is F⌝ and ⌜D is F⌝ differ in meaning, and express different propositions. If n refers to a man m, then, Kripke suggests, ⌜n is F⌝ has the same semantic content as ⌜that man is F⌝, used in a context in which 'that man' demonstratively picks out m.[6] This suggests (i) that even when the reference of n is fixed by description, ⌜n is F⌝ expresses a singular proposition, and (ii) that if p is expressed by ⌜n is F⌝, then, in order to know p one must know, of the referent of n, that it has the property expressed by F. But surely, if this is true of names that have their referents fixed by description, it is also true of those that don't. Since Kripke thinks that most ordinary names are thoroughly nondescriptive in this way, his discussion invites the further inference that the meanings of such names are their referents. However, he never unequivocally endorses this view.[7]

Kripke's verdict on weak descriptivism is mixed. Although he thinks that a few names, e.g., 'Jack the Ripper', have their referents fixed by description, he argues that most do not. Speakers do, of course, often associate names with descriptive information. However, this information typically does not determine reference, *as a matter of linguistic rule*. One argument to this effect is a version of the epistemic argument against Corollary 2 of strong descriptivism.

(i) If D semantically fixes the reference of n, then it should be knowable *in virtue of one's linguistic knowledge alone* that ⌜n is F⌝ expresses a truth iff ⌜D is F⌝ does, and hence

---

[6] Kripke (1972), p. 57.

[7] He does, however, argue, in Kripke (1979a), that it is not refuted by objections based on Frege's puzzle.

that if $\ulcorner$n exists$\urcorner$ is true, then $\ulcorner$n is D$\urcorner$ is also true—since if $\ulcorner$D exists$\urcorner$ is true, then $\ulcorner$D is D$\urcorner$ is too.

(ii) These metalinguistic claims are not so knowable when n is a name like 'Aristotle', or 'Gödel', and D is a description involving well-known accomplishments or characteristics.

(iii) Hence, the referents of these names are not fixed by such descriptions.

Premise (i) reflects the fact that weak descriptivism is a theory about a putative aspect of meaning, mastered by competent speakers, by which the reference of certain terms is defined. To say that *the referent of n is fixed by D*, in the sense of weak descriptivism, is *not* to make the innocuous claim that D played an instrumental role in introducing n and identifying its referent. It is to make a contentious claim about reference-determining information one must possess in order to understand and competently use it. Premise (ii) is based on the observation that one can understand and use a name like 'Gödel', even if one has no accurate information about his accomplishments. What most speakers know is something about his incompleteness theorems. However, one could competently use the name to refer to the same man that everyone else does, even if (a) one knew him by name as a child, and never learned of his work in logic, or (b) one knew about him only that he proved the incompleteness theorems, while knowing about the incompleteness theorems, not what they stated, but only that he proved them. In case (b), one has no descriptive information that simultaneously picks out both the man and the theorems, and hence no fully descriptive, noncircular information that picks out either. There are even cases of successful use in which one's information picks out someone other than Gödel, as illustrated by Kripke's fanciful case in which we discover that Gödel didn't really prove the theorems, but stole them from his colleague Schmidt. In such a case, we would correctly say, "Despite what we previously thought, Gödel didn't prove the incompleteness theorems after all." Since this remark would be patently absurd, and false by definition, if the referent of our use of the name was fixed by the description 'the prover of the incompleteness theorems', its referent isn't so fixed. Nor is it fixed by the description 'the one to whom the incompleteness theorems are generally attributed', unless there is an *independent* way of determining to whom one attributes them when one gives the answer "Gödel did" to the question "Who proved the theorems?"

In sum, the main points in Kripke's discussion of weak descriptivism are the following.

(i) Speakers' information about the referents of names is often incomplete, and sometimes inaccurate. When parasitic descriptions (which define one person's reference in terms of the reference of others) are excluded, and the associated descriptions are limited to the well-known characteristics variety, speakers often successfully use names to refer to things that the descriptions they associate with them do not pick out.

(ii) Even when speakers' information about reference is accurate, and the descriptions given in answer to the question $\ulcorner$To what do you use n to refer?$\urcorner$ are correct, sometimes these answers are circular, or ungrounded, because the descriptions contain other names for which they cannot give noncircular, reference-fixing descriptions. In such cases, the descriptive information possessed by speakers does not uniquely determine reference.

(iii) Even when speakers have a description D that correctly and noncircularly denotes the referent of n, they typically don't know *just by understanding* n that if $\ulcorner$n exists$\urcorner$ is true, then $\ulcorner$n is D$\urcorner$ is also true. Thus, it is not part of the meaning of n that its referent is fixed by D.

The position is strengthened by the fact that thoroughly descriptive, noncircular reference-fixers that are guaranteed to secure correct reference are generally unavailable, *even if parasitic descriptions are allowed*. The point is illustrated by the following table of candidate reference-fixers of the name ('Peano') of the Italian mathematician to whom Dedekind's axiomatization of arithmetic is often attributed.

Description	Reason for Failure
the one who formalized arithmetic	Inaccurate: Dedekind formalized arithmetic
the one to whom the formalization is attributed by most people	Circular when most have no independent way of identifying who that is
the one to whom most refer when they use 'Peano'	Ditto
the one to whom most Peano-experts refer when they use 'Peano'	Who are Peano experts?
the person to whom most mathematicians refer when they use 'Peano'	No guarantee that most mathematicians have the necessary identifying information
the referent of 'Peano' in English	Presupposes that reference in English has already been determined independently

How then is reference typically determined? Kripke's picture is simple. After a name is introduced by some sort of baptism, those who introduced it are able to use it to refer to its bearer. New people pick up the name in conversation and use it themselves, with the reference it has already acquired. The chain of reference transmission grows, as the name is passed from one speaker to the next, each intending to maintain whatever reference it already has. Often, some descriptive information accompanies the passing of the name, but this varies from speaker to speaker, and may, or may not, be accurate. As a result, some may come to associate more inaccurate than accurate information with the name. This doesn't change reference, since reference is determined communally, rather than by the information that individual speakers happen to associate with it.

The picture is, of course, an incomplete sketch. For example, despite the emphasis on reference *inheritance*, sometimes the referent of a name changes without anyone intending it, due to unrecognized conflicts in speakers' intentions—as when speakers, over a period of time, intend to use the name to refer both to what it has designated all along, and to a particular item of their current acquaintance, wrongly taking them to be one and the same. Kripke's picture is too general to provide definite answers to questions of what refers to what in all cases of this sort.[8] It does, however, express a piece of common sense that most speakers implicitly recognize. Might it, then, provide the reference-fixing description required by weak descriptivism?[9] Standardly one intends one's use of a name n to inherit the referent n has already acquired. Given any such use, one could, therefore, correctly (if uninformatively) describe one's intended referent as *"the referent of those previous uses of n, whichever they may be, from which my present use (somehow) inherits its referent."* However, this won't save weak descriptivism, which requires not just any description that picks out the referent of (a use of) n, but a description satisfaction of which is *the means by which* reference is, *as a matter of linguistic rule*, determined. Since the above description denotes the referent of a use of n only if that use has inherited its referent independently, satisfaction of the description can't play this role.

If weak descriptivism is incorrect for most names, what does determine reference? It is tempting to answer, "Baptisms, plus chains of reference transmission." Although there is a sense in which this is correct, there is also a sense in which it isn't. The sense in which it is correct is that baptisms are standard means by which names are introduced, and chains of reference transmission are the means by which new speakers come to use names with the referents they have previously acquired. The sense in which the answer is incorrect is one in which the question asks for some aspect of meaning, distinct from reference, that determines the referents of names. When the question is understood in this way, it falsely presupposes that there is a reference-determining

---

[8] See Berger (2002) for a useful discussion.

[9] The view that (something like) it does is known as *causal descriptivism*. See Searle (1983) chapter 9, Kroon (1987), Lewis (1997) n. 22, Jackson (1998b), and Chalmers (2002). For criticism see Soames (2005a) pp. 297–302 and (2007b) pp. 37–39.

aspect of the meaning of a name. Baptisms and chains of reference transmission help explain how names come to have the meaning/ reference they do, and how that meaning/reference is maintained over time throughout a linguistic community. This is not a special fact about names. Standardly, when one uses any word, one does so with the intention that it should carry whatever meaning and reference it has already acquired in one's linguistic community. This is a fact about the use of all expressions, not about the meanings of any.[10]

4.23 *Natural Kind Terms*

Although 'natural kind term' and 'natural kind' are standardly left undefined, there is general agreement that 'water', 'heat', 'tiger', 'gold', 'cat', and 'green' are such terms, and so designate such kinds. Kripke's theses about them parallel those about proper names. In *Naming and Necessity*, he says "*The original concept of cat is: that kind of thing, where the kind can be identified by paradigmatic instances. It is not something picked out by any qualitative dictionary definition.*"(122). Just as proper names are often introduced by stipulating that they are to apply to objects with which one is acquainted, so terms like 'green' and 'gold' are often introduced by stipulating that they are to designate natural kinds with which we are acquainted through their instances. Such a kind (a color, substance, etc.) is something that can exist at different world-states even if its instances vary from state to state. Kripke also seems to assume that natural kinds are individuated by their instances; a and b are different kinds iff there are metaphysically possible world-states in which their instances differ.

G illustrates the kind of stipulation used to introduce a natural kind term.

> G. The general term 'green' is to designate the color of all, or nearly all, paradigmatic 'green'-samples (and none, or nearly none, of the paradigmatic non-'green'-samples)—i.e. it is to designate the characteristic of object surfaces that is causally responsible for the fact that paradigmatic 'green'-

[10] See pp. 366–71 of Soames (2003b).

samples appear the same way to us (and different from paradigmatic non-'green'-samples). Hence, the predicate 'is green' applies (at w) to objects the surfaces of which have the characteristic which, in @, causally explains why 'green'-samples look the same to us (and different from non-'green'-samples.)

This stipulation is, of course, idealized. 'Green' could have been introduced by G, and it behaves pretty much as it would if it had been. However, it need not have been introduced by formal stipulation. It's enough if speakers started calling things they saw 'green', with the intention that it was to apply to everything of the same color as those things. It makes sense to introduce general terms in this way when three prerequisites are satisfied.

P1. The objects to which we wish to apply the term are similar in some respects, which guide our ordinary application of the term, and allow us, fallibly, but reasonably reliably, to apply it to new cases.

P2. We correctly believe these similarities to have a single unifying explanation, which, although we typically don't know it, we take to involve counterfactual-supporting generalizations relating unknown explanatory features of most similar-appearing samples to the respects in which they are similar.

P3. We wish to use the term in law-like generalizations and explanations, and so don't want to identify its semantic content with the cluster of observed similarities.

Satisfaction of P1 allows us to use the term consistently prior to discovering the unknown explanatory property that its use is intended to track. Satisfaction of P2 and P3 makes the term something more than a tool for noting observed similarities, and results in its designating the initially unknown explanatory property that the term is intended to pick out.[11]

---

[11] The discussion in the text is about semantic values of natural kind terms when the presuppositions governing their introduction and use are satisfied. What values they have when these presuppositions are not satisfied is discussed in chapter 10 of Soames (2002), and on pp. 64–68 of Soames (2005a).

Simple natural kind terms introduced in this way are rigid designators. In the case of 'green', the physics of color, together with G, tell us that it designates a certain property of object surfaces involving proportions of light-waves reflected at different frequencies. Call this property 'SSR_{green}'. Since, 'green' rigidly designates this property, it is a necessary truth that green = SSR_{green}. Two observations support this. (i) A possible world-state w at which both light and the surfaces of objects are just as they are at @ is one at which the same things are green as are green at @, even if our sensory perception at w differs from our perception at @, so that green things at w don't look similar to us, or perhaps are indistinguishable from blue things. (ii) A world-state w at which nothing has SSR_{green} is one in which no surfaces are green—no matter how they might appear to agents, and no matter what surfaces, if any, they call 'green' in their language.

Since 'green' is rigid, it is not synonymous with any nonrigid description. Nor is it synonymous with any 'actually'-rigidified description (for the same reasons as before). Since it is also not synonymous with 'SSR_{green}' (which is short for a complex scientific description of the kind), or with any description of a different kind, strong descriptivism fails for 'green'. Weak descriptivism does too. Since there is no description D which (i) is associated with 'green' by everyone who understands the term, and (ii) is such that $\ulcorner\forall x$ (x is green iff x is D)$\urcorner$ is knowable in virtue of one's linguistic knowledge alone, independent of further empirical evidence, the reference of 'green' is not semantically fixed by description. The same points hold for 'water', 'heat', 'gold', and other natural kind terms. Thus, simple natural kind terms are like proper names in being rigid and nondescriptional, as well as in being introduced by baptisms and acquired through chains of reference transmission.

What do these terms mean? As with proper names, Kripke strongly inclines toward, without explicitly endorsing, the Millian view that there is nothing more to their meanings than their referents. The semantic properties of the predicate $\ulcorner$is k$\urcorner$, where k is a simple natural kind term, are different from, but determined by, those of k. Whereas 'green' rigidly designates the color green—which is both its extension and (given Millianism) its semantic content—'is green' designates the set of things of that color, which is its extension. Since the set of green things varies from world-state to world-state, the predicate is nonrigid. Its meaning consists of the meaning of 'green', together with the contribution of the copula—which indicates that the color is *predicated* of its argument. In effect, the meaning of 'is green' is the property *being green* (which, when the predicate occurs in a sentence, is predicated of something).[12]

4.24 *Kripke's Essentialist Route to the Necessary Aposteriori*

Let p be a true proposition that attributes an n-place property (relation) F to an object o (or series of objects), conditional on the object (or objects) existing—while not attributing further properties to anything. Then, p will be an instance of the necessary *aposteriori* if (a) F is an essential property of o if F is a property of o at all (similarly for a series of objects),[13] (b) knowledge of o that it has F, if it exists, can only be had *aposteriori* (similarly for the series), and (c) knowing p involves knowing of o that it has F, if it exists at all (similarly for the series).[14] Similar rules generate instances of the necessary aposteriori that are negations of propositions attributing properties to objects that they *couldn't* have had, propositions that are universal generalizations of conditionals, the consequents of which attribute properties that are essential to every possible object that satisfies the antecedent, and so on. Given the needed metaphysical claims about which properties are essential to which objects, one can use such recipes to generate all unproblematic instances of the Kripkean necessary aposteriori.[15]

---

[12] See Soames (forthcoming b) for further discussion.

[13] Often, it seems to be possible to know that (a) is satisfied by knowing apriori of F that it is an essential property of anything that has it (or that it essentially relates any objects it actually relates).

[14] To generate instances of the necessary aposteriori like 'Noman is human, if he exists' about a merely possible man, while avoiding a similar characterization of 'Noman is a cat, if he exists', (b) must be changed to read *knowledge of o that it would have F, if it were to exist, can be had, but only aposteriori.* Thanks to Teresa Robertson.

[15] Soames (2006; forthcoming a).

5a. Kripke is a human being, if Kripke exists.

b. This table is made of molecules, if this table exists.

c. Kripke = the individual who developed from sperm a and egg b (if Kripke exists).

λx [$\forall y$ (y developed from sperm a and egg b $\leftrightarrow$ y = x)] Kripke (if Kripke exists)

d. Water = the substance instances of which are made up molecules with two hydrogen atoms and one oxygen atom (if water exists).

λx [$\forall y$ (y is a substance with molecular structure H_2O $\leftrightarrow$ y = x)] water (if water exists)

6a. Kripke isn't a robot.

b. This table isn't a human being.

c. Kaplan $\neq$ Kripke

7a. Cats are animals.

$\forall x$ (x is a cat $\supset$ x is an animal)

b. Lightning is electricity.

$\forall x$ [x is (an instance of) lightning $\supset$ x is (an instance of) electricity]

c. Light is a stream of photons.

$\forall x$ [x is (an instance of) light $\supset$ x is a stream of photons]

d. Heat is mean molecular kinetic energy.

$\forall x \forall y$ [x is hotter than y $\leftrightarrow$ the mean molecular kinetic energy of x is greater than that of y]

e. Water is H_2O and ice is too.

$\forall x$ [x is (an instance of) water $\supset$ x is (an instance of) H_2O] & $\forall x$ [x is (an instance of) ice $\supset$ x is (an instance of) H_2O]

The only putative examples of the Kripkean necessary aposteriori that can't be generated in this way are identities, like those in (8), involving linguistically simple names or natural kind terms.

8a. Mark Twain = Samuel Clemens

b. Woodchucks are groundhogs (and vice versa). / $\forall x$ (x is a woodchuck $\leftrightarrow$ x is a groundhog)

If we try to apply the formula for generating instances of the necessary aposteriori to (8a), we find that although an object and itself are indeed *essentially* related by identity, it is *not* knowable only aposteriori that identity so relates any pair (if the pair exists)—since if anything is knowable apriori, it is that o is identical with o. Essentially the same point can be made about the kinds in (8b). Thus we *cannot* use the standard Kripkean formula to characterize (8a) and (8b) as instances of the necessary aposteriori. Of course, this doesn't show that there is no other route to this conclusion—and indeed Kripke himself thought that there was. However, as argued in Soames (2006) and Soames (forthcoming a), this was a mistake. Finally, it can be argued that, despite appearances, these sentences express propositions that *are* knowable apriori.[16]

4.3 KAPLAN ON DIRECT REFERENCE AND INDEXICALITY

4.31 *Significance: The Tension between Logic and Semantics*

David Kaplan's "Demonstratives: An Essay on the Semantics, Logic, Metaphysics and Epistemology of Demonstratives and Other Indexicals" is, along with Kripke (1972) and Montague (1973), one of the three most influential works in the philosophy of language in the last forty years. As the title indicates, it is multifaceted. At its center is a system of logic, complete with formal language, model theory, and definitions of logical truth and consequence. The distinguishing feature of this logic is its inclusion of terms the interpretations of which vary from one context of utterance to another. This is a striking development in a logical tradition a central aim of which has been to construct precise, mechanically checkable, systems for reasoning sufficient for mathematics and science, by eliminating those features of natural language—vast syntactical variety, ambiguity, context sensitivity, and indexicality—that seem to stand in the way. Kaplan's logic shows that indexicality can be accommodated. There is, however, a puzzle about the significance of this achievement. Indexicality isn't needed in formalizations of mathematics and science. Nor is formalization required for most ordinary reasoning we do with indexicals in natural language. What then is a logic of indexicals

---

[16] See Salmon (1984).

good for? As Kaplan's title suggests, its chief value lies in what it teaches us about the meaning and use of natural language indexicals. However, it is at precisely this point that we encounter a tension. As we shall see, some features of his system, designed to further the goal of logical formalization, are semantically significant departures from natural language. In particular, the semantics of natural-language demonstratives differ in important ways from those of their Kaplanean counterparts, making the extraction of crucial lessons more difficult.

4.32 The Basic Structure of the Logic of Demonstratives

We start with a formal language LD, sentences of which are evaluated at different times t and world-states w. A model M for LD specifies sets of times, world-states, and possible individuals, a domain of which is assigned to each <t,w>. M also assigns an *intension* to each nonlogical symbol, which is a function from such pairs to *extensions*. Since names are rigid, their intensions determine the same extension at each <t,w>. The extensions of n-place predicates, which typically vary from one <t,w> to the next, are sets of n-tuples to which the predicates apply. The intension of a sentence ⌜Pn⌝ is a function that assignees truth (falsity) to a pair <t,w> iff the extension of n at <t,w> is (isn't) a member of the extension of P at <t,w>. The intensions of complex sentences, relative to M, are similarly determined.

LD also has *intensional operators* the extensions of which map the intensions of their (sentential) arguments onto truth values. Examples include ⌜*Necessarily/Possibly* S⌝ and ⌜In the *future/past* it *will be/was* the case that S⌝. The truth values of these sentences at <t,w> depend on the truth values of S at other world-states or times. What is it to evaluate S at such a pair? One answer is that it is to take S to be true at <t,w> iff S would express a truth if used at t,w (with the same meaning it has here and now). A different answer is that it is to take S to be true at <t,w> iff *what S expresses* (as used here and now) would be true were w to obtain at t. With nonindexical sentences, it doesn't matter which answer we accept.

When indexicals like 'now' are considered, it does.

9a. In the future it will be the case that *the person who is F* is G.

b. In the future it will be the case that *the person who is now F* is G.

Imagine both sentences used at a context C consisting of time t_C and world-state w_C. (9a) (used at C) is true (at C) iff there is a later time t+ at which the person who is F *then* is G; (9b) (used at C) is true (at C) iff there is a later time t+ at which the person who is F *at* t_C is G. To get these results—while keeping the descriptions in the scope of the future tense operator—we must keep track of the time of C while evaluating the embedded sentence at t+. The truth of (9b) (used at C) requires the truth at t+ of (9c) (remembering it was used at C), which requires the denotation at t+ of (9d) to be G then.[17]

9c. *The person who is now F is G.*

d. the x: Now Fx

In LD, definite descriptions are complex singular terms ⌜the x: Sx⌝ which denote, at <t,w>, the unique satisfier of Sx at <t,w> (if there is one). So, the denotation at t+ of (9d) (as used at C) is the unique object o such that (9e) (so used) is true at t+ relative to an assignment of o to 'x'.

9e. Now Fx

To get the desired truth conditions, the denotation at t+ of (9d) (as used in C) must be the same as its denotation at t_C—which requires 'Now' to "designate" t_C, and o to satisfy (9e) at t+ iff o is F *at* t_C. The rule R_N—which involves double indexing the truth values of sentences to both the time of the context and a second, potentially different, time of evaluation—yields these results.

R_N ⌜Now S⌝ as used in a context $<t_C,w_C>$ is true when evaluated at an arbitrary time, world-state pair <t,w> iff S as used in $<t_C,w_C>$ is true at $<t_C,w_C>$.

---

[17] 'F' and 'G' are here used as schematic letters, rather than metalinguistic variables.

The modal indexical 'actually' requires the same sort of double indexing.

10a. It could have been the case that *the person who F-ed G-ed.*

  b. It could have been the case that the person who actually *F-ed* G-ed.

(10b) (used in C) is true (at C) iff there is world-state w, possible from w_C, at which the person who is F *at* w_C is G. To get this result—while keeping the description in the scope of the possibility operator—we need to keep track of the designated "actual" world-state of C when evaluating the embedded sentence at w. The rule for 'actually' does this.

R_N ⌜Actually S⌝ as used in a context $<t_C,w_C>$ is true when evaluated at an arbitrary time, world-state pair $<t, w>$ iff S as used in $<t_C,w_C>$ is true at $<t, w_C>$.

Kaplan's model theory evaluates sentences relative to a context C, $<t_C,w_C>$, and a circumstance of evaluation E, $<t,w>$. He interprets the claim that S is true relative to C and E as the claim that, at C, S expresses a proposition p that is true at E (i.e., that would be true were E to obtain). In other words, setting S in C gives us a content—*what S says* in C—about which we can ask whether it would have been true when, or if, other circumstances obtain.

Adding 'I' and 'here' to LD requires adding a designated agent a_C and location l_C to contexts, subject to the constraint that a_C exists, and is located at l_C, at $<t_C,w_C>$.

R_I For all contexts C and circumstances E, the referent of 'I' relative to C, E = a_C.

R_{here} For all contexts C and circumstances E, the referent of 'here' relative to C, E = l_C.

Thus, contexts are quadruples, $<t_C,w_C,a_C,l_C>$, while circumstances remain pairs, $<t,w>$. A model-theoretic semantics for LD is a specification of truth at a context C and circumstance E, for each sentence, extracted from the definition/theory of truth *at arbitrary C, E of a model M*—plus an intended model. Given the semantics, we define *the meaning* of an expression to be a function from contexts C to its intension at C, and the meaning of a sentence S to be a function from contexts C to sets of circumstances at which S, when placed in C, is true. If we identify propositions with sets of circumstances, we have a rule that tells us what propositions S expresses at arbitrary contexts. Kaplan calls this *the character of S,* and takes it to be what one knows when one understands S. *The content of S* at C is what S expresses, or semantically encodes, at C. (Similarly for the characters and contents of other expressions.) Of course, Kaplan doesn't really think that propositions are sets of times and world-states. Rather, he is inclined to think of them as structured complexes the constituents of which are the semantic contents of the parts of the sentences that express them. On this attractive picture, the content of S is (really) a structured proposition, and the character of S is (really) a function from contexts to such propositions. The model-theoretic semantics only approximates this reality.

4.33 *Direct Reference and Rigid Designation*

The difference between approximation and reality affects how we understand the relationship between direct reference and rigid designation, which are defined as follows.

Direct Reference

A singular term t is directly referential iff for all contexts C and assignments A the referent of t with respect to C and A = the semantic content of t with respect to C and A. The referent of a directly referential term t with respect to a context C, assignment A, and circumstance of evaluation E, is the content of t with respect to C and A.

Generalized Definition of Rigid Designation

A singular term t is a rigid designator iff for all contexts C, assignments A, circumstances of evaluation E, and objects o, if t refers to o with respect to C, A, and E, then t refers to o with respect to C, A, and E', for all circumstances E' in which o exists, and t never refers to anything else with respect to C, A, and any circumstance E*.

Contextualized Rigid Designation

A singular term t is a rigid designator with respect to a context C and assignment A iff there is an object o such that (i) t refers to o with respect to C, A, and the world-state w_C and time t_C of C, and (ii) for all circumstances of evaluation E in which o exists, t refers to o with respect to C, A, and E, and (iii) t never refers to anything else with respect to C, A, and any circumstance E*.

If t is directly referential, t must be rigid. However, the converse doesn't hold. Whereas 'the cube root of 343' and 'the one who actually wrote *Naming and Necessity*' are rigid, their contents are not their referents, but rather are descriptive conditions that determine the same referent at every circumstance. The contrast between these descriptions and terms that are genuinely directly referential—e.g., 'I' and individual variables—is illustrated by (11) and (12).

11a. The cube root of 343 is F.
  b. x is F. (relative to an assignment of 7 to 'x')
12a. The x: actually x wrote *Naming and Necessity* is F.
  b. x is F. (relative to an assignment of Kripke to 'x')
  c. I am F. (said by Kripke)

In order to believe the proposition expressed by (11a), it isn't necessary to believe, of 7, that it is F, but it is necessary to believe that whatever number yields 343 when cubed is F. The situation is reversed for (11b). To believe what it expresses, one must believe, of 7, that it is F, though no specific descriptive belief is required. The same contrast is found in (12). These facts follow naturally from the thesis that the semantic contents of rigid descriptions are descriptive conditions, whereas those of 'I' and 'x' are their referents, relative to contexts C and assignments A.[18] Unfortunately, this distinction is lost in the model theory, according to which the content of any term t, relative to C and A, is t's model-theoretic intension relative to C and A—which, when t is rigid, is always a constant function from circumstances of evaluation to t's un-

[18] Again, 'F' is here used as a schematic letter.

changing referent. Thus, Kaplan's crucial distinction between the general notion of rigid designation and the special case of direct reference requires structured semantic contents not provided by his model theory.

4.34 'Dthat' and 'Actually'

With this in mind, we introduce a second Kaplanean indexical that can be used to rigidify a description. Unlike 'actually', which combines with formulas to form formulas, 'dthat' combines with singular terms, including definite descriptions, to form singular terms.

R_{dthat} The referent of $\ulcorner$dthat[a]$\urcorner$ at a context C and circumstance E is the referent of a at C, t_C, w_C. $\ulcorner$Dthat [the x: Fx]$\urcorner$ is a *directly referential* term the content of which, at C, is the object denoted by $\ulcorner$the x: Fx$\urcorner$ at C, t_C, w_C (if there is one). This object is the referent of the term at C and E, for all E—whether or not it exists at E.

Although both 'dthat' and 'actually' are rigidifiers, 'actually'-rigidified descriptions are never directly referential, while 'dthat'-rigidified descriptions always are. 'Dthat' is syncategorematic. Having no semantic content of its own, it merely converts non-directly referential terms to directly referential ones. By contrast, the content of 'actually' at C is the property *being true at* w_C, just as the content of 'now' at C is *being true at* t_C. The proposition q expressed by $\ulcorner$Actually S$\urcorner$ at C predicates *being true at* w_C of the proposition p expressed by S. So, q is true at arbitrary t,w iff p is true at $<t,w_C>$, and whenever p is true at $<t_C,w_C>$, q is true at $<t_C,w>$, for all w. Similarly, when $\ulcorner$the x: Fx$\urcorner$ denotes a unique individual o at C, $\ulcorner$the x: actually Fx$\urcorner$ denotes o with respect to C and all world-states at which o exists, while never denoting anything else at other world-states. Hence, 'actually' is sometimes a rigidifier.[19] However, the resulting descriptions aren't directly

---

[19] There are limitations on when 'actually' rigidifies a description—when the domains of quantifiers, and Kaplan's operator 'the', are allowed to vary from one world-state to another. Suppose $\ulcorner$the x: Fx$\urcorner$ fails to designate an

referential. If $\lceil$the x: Fx$\rceil$ and $\lceil$the x: Gx$\rceil$ are contingently code-signative, then $\lceil$the x: actually Fx$\rceil$ and $\lceil$the x: actually Gx$\rceil$ rigidly designate the same thing, while having different (descriptive) semantic contents—which are also expressed by $\lceil$the unique object that is F at $w_c\rceil$ and $\lceil$the unique object that is G at $w_c\rceil$. Since, on the structured conception, the contents of these descriptions contain the distinct contents of their nonrigid counterparts, the two 'actually'-rigidified descriptions differ in content. By contrast, any pair of coreferential '*dthat*'-rigidified descriptions have the same semantic contents.

4.35 *English Demonstratives vs. 'Dthat'-Rigidified Descriptions*

'Dthat' aside, we have so far considered the indexicals 'now' and 'actually', 'I' and 'here'. The former are represented by sentential operators in the logic of demonstratives; the latter by singular terms. This works fine for 'actually', but it is a simplification for 'now', which can also occur in English as a singular term, as in 'Now is the time for action'. The same can be said about 'yesterday', 'today', and 'tomorrow'—all of which can be understood as having both operator and singular term uses. Kaplan represents 'yesterday' by a sentential operator modeled on his 'Now'-operator; similar operators representing 'today' and 'tomorrow' could easily

---

object at w_c of C because more than one object existing at w_c has the property expressed by F. Suppose further that there are two such objects, o_1 and o_2, that o_1 exists at w_1 but not at w_2, and that o_2 exists at w_2 but not w_1. In comparing what $\lceil$the x: actually Fx$\rceil$ designates relative to C, and w_1 with what it designates relative to C and w_2, one must remember that the uniqueness condition carried by 'the' is imposed not on w_c, but on the world-state of the circumstance of evaluation. $\lceil$The x: actually Fx$\rceil$ designates o relative to C and w iff o is the unique object existing at w which, at w_c, has the property expressed by F. Since it designates o_1 at C,w_1, while designating o_2 at C,w_2, it isn't rigid. In cases like these, $\lceil$the x: actually Fx$\rceil$ doesn't satisfy the generalized definition of rigid designation, though it may satisfy the contextualized definition, depending on the context.

be added. In these cases, the simplifications of Kaplan's system don't seriously diminish its semantic significance for English.[20]

Kaplan treats *pure indexicals*—like 'I', 'now', 'actually', and 'today'—as each having a constant linguistic meaning (character), known by competent speakers, which determines different semantic contents in different contexts. Since these contents are objective features of the context (agent, time, world-state, and day of the time of the context)—a use of one of these expressions in C will carry the content provided by C, with no need of special beliefs or intentions on the part of the speaker to determine that content. So long as I intend to use 'I' and 'today' with their conventional meanings, they will refer to me, and the day of my utterance, and not to Saul Kripke and some other day d*—even if I wrongly take myself to be Saul Kripke, and the day of my utterance to be d*, and intend my uses of the terms to refer to them. Such intentions are irrelevant to determining the referents/contents of pure indexicals.

Thus, it is natural that different occurrences of the same pure indexical (e.g., 'I' or 'yesterday') will determine the same referent/content in a single context. Since a context provides only one agent/speaker, and only one time, the result couldn't be otherwise. In actual conversation, it is, of course, possible for different speakers to utter different sentences, or even for one speaker to

---

[20] Two issues are more serious. First, Kaplan simplifies the semantics of 'now' by always assigning it one of the basic units of time provided by the model, whereas in English 'now' can pick out an instant, an hour, a year, etc. In light of this, it is not clear that 'now' should be treated as a "pure indexical" (the interpretation of which in a context doesn't require a "demonstration"), as opposed to a demonstrative the content of which is some period of time determined by the intentions of the speaker that must include, but not necessarily be limited to, the designated moment of the context. The same issue arises with 'here', which has a demonstrative use (in which it contrasts with the demonstrative 'there'). Second, it is questionable whether indexicals like 'yesterday'—and, by extension, 'yesteryear', and 'yester-century'—are directly referential, as opposed to being *defined* in terms of other directly referential expressions such as 'the day before *today*', 'the year before *this year*', etc. See Kripke (2008).

interrupt and finish another's sentence. It is also possible to start a discourse on one day, and finish it on the next. For these reasons, real discourses can contain multiple occurrences of pure indexicals with different referents/contents. This discrepancy between real-life speech situations and Kaplan's system should be regarded as an idealization. Although we will return to this point in chapter 7 in the course of examining a different, perhaps more realistic, semantic account of English indexicals, the point to notice here is that the idealization is all but forced on him by his goal of developing *a logic* for indexicals. For, it is natural to think, any putative logic in which the transition from A and ⌜A ⊃ B⌝ to B sometimes failed to preserve truth, because different occurrences of the same expression in A or B received different interpretations, would scarcely count as a logic at all.

The same can't be said for Kaplan's treatment of genuine demonstratives—like 'he', 'she', 'you', 'this', and 'that'. Although the point just made about *modus ponens* applies to them too, it is commonplace for different occurrences of a genuine demonstrative in a sentence or discourse to refer to different things. This is connected to another difference between demonstratives and pure indexicals. Expressions of both kinds have context-invariant meanings, mastered by competent speakers, that (partially) determine different referents/contents in different contexts. However, whereas the referents/contents of pure indexicals are determined by objective features of the context, independent of specific referential intentions of speakers, the referents/contents of demonstratives *are* determined, in part, by such intentions. These content-determining intentions vary not only from one context to the next, but also from one *occurrence* to the next, *within the same context* (where by 'context' I here mean a situation in which expressions are used in speech, or in thought).

These features of English demonstratives can't be accommodated in the logic of demonstratives, as Kaplan views it. Since he (quite naturally) defines *logical truth* to be truth at all contexts of all models, and *logical consequence* to be truth at all contexts of all models at which the entailing premises are true, he can't accommodate expressions different occurrences of which have different referents/contents in the same context—while retaining such commonplace laws as 'S ⊃ S', and such compelling rules as *modus ponens*. Nor, if his logic is to be formal, can he rely on hidden and varying speaker intentions to provide interpretations of expressions in his logical language. Faced with these realities, Kaplan had to make a choice: either to give up the project of providing a formal logic of demonstratives (as he conceived it), and concentrate instead on providing an accurate semantics for English indexicals and demonstratives, or to abandon such a semantics in favor of a logic in which English demonstratives are *replaced* by formal counterparts useful in *regimenting* and *modeling* ordinary indexical reasoning. He chose the latter.

The referent of an occurrence of an English demonstrative is constrained by the meaning of the demonstrative. Typically, 'he' is constrained to refer to a male, 'she' to a female, 'you' to one who is being addressed, 'we' to some group that includes the speaker, 'they' to some group that doesn't, ⌜that F⌝ to something that satisfies F, and 'that' to something nonhuman. Since this is usually not enough to determine a (unique) referent, speakers' referential intentions, supplemented, in some cases, by overt demonstrations—pointings, nods, gestures—are also required. Kaplan introduces a technical sense of the term "demonstration" to cover this motley collection of reference-determining factors. He makes the further assumption that in any given case, a demonstration δ will have a content of some sort that specifies a condition to be satisfied by the referent of (the occurrence of) the English demonstrative d plus δ. That content combines with the meaning of d to provide a content that determines the referent, if any, of (the occurrence of) d plus δ in the context. Next he imagines finding a definite description D that expresses that reference-determining content. ⌜Dthat D⌝ is then the term of LD that replaces (the occurrence of) d supplemented by δ. Like other indexicals in LD, (i) it has a context-invariant meaning that returns different contents in different contexts (when D is nonrigid), (ii) it is directly referential, (iii) its content in a context C is determined by objective features of C, without further reference to speaker intentions, and (iv) different occurrences of it must have the same content in C. The end result is an infinite set of 'dthat' terms, each of which represents a possible use of an English demonstrative.

4.36 *Final Assessment*

Kaplan's logic of demonstratives can be evaluated by the extent to which the logical properties of arguments formulated in LD correspond to our pretheoretic assessments of sound and unsound deductive reasoning with English indexicals. Although such an assessment is a delicate and complicated matter, it is pretty clear that his logic should receive high marks. Among its broadly significant philosophical lessons, illustrated by (13), is the existence of sentences which, though merely contingent, are logically, or analytically, true.

13. $(S \leftrightarrow \text{Actually, Now } S)$, Now (Located, I, here), $(\exists x \; x = [\text{the } y : Dy] \supset \text{dthat } [\text{the } y : Dy] = [\text{the } y : Dy])$

Stripped of technicalities, the point is simply that a sentence can be guaranteed, logically (or analytically), to express a truth, even if the truth (i.e., proposition) it expresses isn't necessary.[21] However, despite the importance of this point—as well as the success of the logic as a regimentation of our indexical reasoning, and its insights about the meanings of pure indexicals—Kaplan's system does not provide the basis for an adequate semantic model for English demonstratives. Even if every use of such a demonstrative can, for purposes of regimentation, be represented by a 'dthat' term, nothing in LD corresponds to the demonstratives themselves. Unlike 'dthat', which is syncategorematic, the demonstratives themselves have contextually invariant meanings, and contextually varying referents. Unlike 'dthat'-rigidified descriptions, the referents of real demonstratives are typically dependent on speakers' intentions, and different occurrences of them can refer to different things in the same context of utterance. Thus, one of

---

[21] There are also lessons to be learned about the relationship between indexicality, apriority, analyticity, and logical truth. See Soames (2005a) pp. 44–54, 66, and Soames (2007a) for discussion.

the chief problems that Kaplan's model was designed to answer—namely, providing a semantics for demonstratives in natural language—remains unsolved.

Selected Further Reading

Chalmers, David (2002), "On Sense and Intension."
Jackson, Frank (1998a), *From Metaphysics to Ethics.*
Kaplan, David (1989a), "Demonstratives."
——— (1989b), "Afterthoughts."
Kripke, Saul (1972), *Naming and Necessity.*
——— (1979a), "A Puzzle about Belief."
Putnam, Hilary (1970), "Is Semantics Possible?"
——— (1973), "Explanation and Reference."
——— (1975), "The Meaning of 'Meaning.'"
Salmon, Nathan (1981), *Reference and Essence.*
——— (2002), "Demonstrating and Necessity."
Soames, Scott (2005a), Reference and Description.

PART TWO

New Directions

The Metaphysics of Meaning: Propositions and Possible Worlds

5.1 LOCI OF CONTROVERSY

Apart from truth and reference, no notions are more central to theories of meaning and the philosophy of language than *proposition* and *possible world*. However, they are also sources of controversy. Propositions are bearers of truth, semantic contents of sentences, and that which we assert, believe, and know. Possible worlds—aka *ways the world could have been*—are parameters to which truth is relativized. The controversy about propositions and possible worlds concerns whether they exist at all, what sorts of things they are (if they do exist), and which, if either, is explanatorily fundamental. For some, e.g., Davidson, theories of language don't require either one, and their existence is doubtful. For others, e.g., Lewis and Stalnaker, possible worlds are fundamental, and propositions are sets of worlds. For still others, e.g., Robert Adams, propositions are fundamental, and possible worlds are sets of propositions.[1] In this chapter, I indicate what I take propositions and possible worlds to be, and sketch their roles in theorizing.

First we need to clear up a common confusion encouraged by substituting the shorthand terminology 'possible worlds' for the more accurate '*ways the world could possibly be, or have been*'. Outside philosophy, when we speak of "the world," we often mean the Earth. People say "We want to travel around the world," meaning that they want to travel around the Earth. But 'the world' can also

---

[1] Adams, (1974), Davidson (1967), (1970); Lewis (1979), (1986); Stalnaker (1984).

be used to designate the universe as a whole—a massive concrete entity, of which all other concrete entities are parts. This is how many people interpret philosophical talk about "the actual world." But if the actual world is the universe, it is natural to suppose that possible worlds are different universes. So, when philosophers say that there are other possible worlds, they are often taken to mean that, in addition to the actual universe, there are other universes disconnected from ours, with inhabitants who, though similar to us, are not really us, but our counterparts. According to this picture—misleading called "modal realism"—reality is not the universe; it is the pluriverse.[2]

The metaphysical extravagance of this view provokes resistance. In response, modal realists claim both that modal talk is indispensable, and that possible worlds semantics has shown that modal truths require the existence of possible worlds. Since those who accept these points don't deny modal truths, they feel pressed to admit the existence of possible worlds, despite their doubts.[3] However, "modal realism" is not so easily established. Although modal talk is indispensable, the idea that by analyzing the meanings of ordinary truths involving words like 'could', 'would', and 'possibly', we learn of the existence of alternate universes is a fantasy. We don't mean anything of the sort by our ordinary modal talk, and if we did, we would have no justification for accepting the modal truths we find indispensable. The main errors come from identifying *ways the world could be* with alternate concrete universes, taking possible worlds semantics to give the *meanings* of ordinary modal sentences, and thinking that modal notions can be *analyzed away,* rather than taken as primitive.

---

[2] Lewis (1986).

[3] A related response, pioneered in Rosen (1990), takes worlds to be concrete universes, but treats modal language as embodying a *fiction* about them. On this view, ⌜It is necessary that S⌝ means something like ⌜According to the Lewis-fiction, plus an encyclopedia listing all facts about the actual world, 'S' is true in all concrete universes⌝. Although this avoids ontological commitment to alternate universes, it grants "modal realism" too much priority. The choice is *not* between analyzing modal statements as literally incredible and taking them to be merely fictional.

Each of these points will be addressed in section 5.3. For now, it is enough to identify what *ways the world could be* are. A way something—e.g., my office—could be, but isn't—e.g., tidy—is a property it could have had, but doesn't. Ways the world could be, but isn't, are properties the world could have had but doesn't, while the way the world is, is a property it has.[4] Thus, the proper terminology isn't possible vs. actual *world,* but possible vs. actual *world-state.*

5.2 PROPOSITIONS

5.21 *Why We Need Them and Why Theories of Truth Conditions Can't Provide Them*

Propositions are needed in semantics (i) as referents of names like 'Logicism' and 'Church's Thesis', and of demonstratives in examples like 'That's true', (ii) as entities quantified over in sentences like 'At least six of those theses are unsupported by evidence', and (iii) as objects of attitudes in 'Alex believes the proposition that all men are created equal' and 'Mary defended several claims that Bill denied'. Propositions are also needed to state the goals of semantic theory, and to relate it to the interpretation of speakers. Even if a language lacks attitude verbs, semantics informs us about what speakers assert and believe, when they sincerely utter, or assent to, a sentence. Since propositions are what is asserted and believed, and since semantic content is a prime determinant of those assertions and beliefs, propositions are presupposed by our best account of what semantic theories do.

At 2.3, I argued that Davidsonian truth theories, which shun propositions, don't provide enough information to qualify as theories of meaning. At 3.1 and 3.3, I extended the argument to theories of truth at possible world-states. Although these theories are more informative than Davidson's, they aren't informative enough to allow one who knows them to understand what sentences mean, or to identify the beliefs they express. This shortcoming can't be remedied by finding circumstances relative to

---

[4] See Stalnaker (1976).

which sentences may be evaluated for truth that are more fine-grained than epistemically possible world-states. That was the goal of Barwise and Perry (1983), the failure of which showed that no theory satisfying certain well-motivated assumptions—e.g., that ⌜P&Q⌝ is true at a circumstance E iff both conjuncts are true at E, and ⌜∃x Fx⌝ is true at E iff Fx is true of some object o at E— can identify the semantic contents of sentences (the propositions they express) with functions from circumstances to truth values, no matter how fine-grained the circumstances.[5] Thus, there is no hope of using such truth theories as theories of meaning, or of extracting propositions from them.

This result leads back to Frege and (the early) Russell, who recognized propositions as explanatorily primary. Instead of being extracted from rules determining the truth conditions of S, the proposition S expresses is what its truth conditions are derived from. Being the meaning of S, this proposition encodes, or is composed out of, the meanings of S's constituents. Since truth-conditional intensions (functions from circumstances to extensions) lack this feature, they can't be the meanings of complex expressions, or the propositions expressed by sentences.[6] Hence, the need for an independent theory of propositions.

---

[5] Soames (1987), (2008b).

[6] One approach not ruled out by anything said so far takes meanings of complex expressions to be tree structures, the nodes of which are the truth-conditional intensions of the corresponding constituents. Even then, however, one must allow some syntactically simple constituents to have complex intensional structures—as when 'fortnight' is stipulated to be synonymous with 'a period of 14 days'. One must also find a way of avoiding paradox involving beliefs about beliefs. The intension of 'believe' is a function from circumstances to sets of pairs of an agent and a proposition believed, which on this proposal is a structured intension. Given the set-theoretic account of functions and pairs, we get the paradoxical result that when the intension of 'believe' is a constituent of the structured intension believed, it is a member of a member . . . of itself. Finally, as I argue below, the best account of possible world-states uses objects and properties to explain them; so properties shouldn't be explained in terms of world-states, as they are under this proposal. See Soames (2007a).

5.22 *Why Traditional Propositions Won't Do*

According to Frege and Russell, propositions are meanings of sentences, bearers of truth, and objects of the attitudes. Despite this, both believed there to be a mystery at the heart of the proposition, which they took to be a complex constructed from the meanings of the constituents of a sentence expressing it. Just as sentences aren't mere collections of unrelated expressions, but rather have a structural unity that distinguishes them from a mere list, so propositions aren't mere collections of the meanings of expressions, but rather have a unity that distinguishes them from arbitrary aggregates of their parts. Frege and Russell found this unity mysterious.

Russell put the problem this way.

Consider, for example, the proposition "A differs from B." The constituents of this proposition, if we analyze it, appear to be only A, difference, B. *Yet these constituents, thus placed side by side, do not reconstitute the proposition. The difference which occurs in the proposition actually relates A and B, whereas the difference after analysis is a notion which has no connection with A and B.* It may be said that we ought, in the analysis, to mention the relations which difference has to A and B, relations which are expressed by *is* and *from* when we say A is different from B. These relations consist in the fact that A is referent and B relatum with respect to difference. But A, referent, difference, relatum, B, is still merely a list of terms, not a proposition. *A proposition, in fact, is essentially a unity, and when analysis has destroyed the unity, no enumeration of constituents will restore the proposition. The verb, when used as a verb, embodies the unity of the proposition, and is thus distinguishable from the verb considered as a term, though I do not know how to give a clear account of the precise nature of the distinction.*[7]

Certainly, there is more to the proposition *that A differs from B* than the fact that its constituents are A, B, and difference. There is

---

[7] Russell (1903), 49–50, my emphasis.

also the manner in which the constituents occur. Presumably, this has something to do with the fact that the proposition *predicates* difference of A and B, and so *represents A as being different from B*. Since a list doesn't predicate anything of anything else, it isn't representational.

Is this problematic? Consider sentence (1), in which 'difference' and 'identity' are abstract nouns, 'different' is an adjective that combines with the copula to form a predicate, and 'from difference' is a prepositional phrase modifying the predicate.

1. $[_S [_N$ Difference] $[_{VP} [_V$ is different] $[_{PP} [_P$ from] $[_{NP}$ identity]]]]

The constituents of the proposition expressed by (1) are the relations identity and difference, the latter occurring twice. Understanding (1) involves understanding its words, which provide the proposition's constituents, plus the hierarchical structure in which the words are arranged, which indicates what is predicated of what. Just as one who understands the sentence recognizes one expression as predicate and others as arguments, so, it might be argued, one who entertains the proposition recognizes from its structural configuration which of its constituents is predicated of which. On this view, what distinguishes a proposition from a mere aggregate of constituents parallels what distinguishes a sentence from a mere list. The structural relations that constituents bear to one another carry the information about predication needed for representational content.

But how is this picture filled out? How, exactly, does the arrangement of the constituents of the proposition expressed by (1) show that difference is predicated of difference and identity? Consider some candidates for this proposition.

2a. < difference, <difference, identity> >
 b. { {difference}, {difference, { {difference}, {difference, identity}}}}
 c. < <identity, difference>, difference >
 d. {{{identity}, {identity, difference}}, {{ {identity}, {identity, difference}}, difference }}

3a.

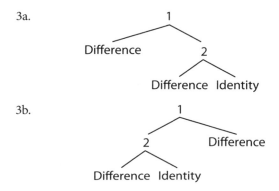

3b.

Although any of these structures could serve as a formal model of the proposition expressed by (1), none could be that proposition. Remember, the proposition *represents difference as being different from identity*, because it *predicates* difference of difference and identity. Since there is nothing in (2), (3), or any other formal structure we might specify that, *by its very nature*, indicates that anything is predicated of anything, such structures are neither intrinsically representational nor capable of being true or false.

We could, if we wished, *adopt* rules that would allow us to read off information about predication from the structures, and so *interpret* them. However, this would *not* make them propositions in the traditional sense. Such propositions are *not* things to which we *give meanings*. They *are* the meanings we assign to sentences, when we interpret them. The real problem with Russell's discussion is his assumption that propositions are intrinsically representational, independent of us, and also that from which the representational features of our cognitive states and sentences are inherited. Since this assumption makes it impossible to answer the question "*What makes propositions representational?*," there are no Russellian propositions.

The same conclusion holds for Fregean propositions, which are also assumed to be representational independent of us. Frege differs from Russell in postulating "unsaturated" senses that are intrinsically predicative, and so always occur in a predicative

115

role.[8] Although this may sound attractive, it isn't, since it leads him to conclude that neither the sense nor referent of any predicative expression can be designated by a nonpredicative expression—and, thereby, made the subject of a further predication. This thesis—that if Pred is a predicate, then *the sense of Pred* is unsaturated, *the referent of Pred* is incomplete, and neither can be designated by any nonpredicative expression—is self-defeating, as shown by the italicized phrases used in stating it.[9]

5.23 *Toward a Naturalistic Theory of Propositions*

Since we need propositions in our linguistic and cognitive theories, the failure of traditional conceptions calls for a new conception that reverses explanatory priorities. Propositions are *not* the source of representationality in mind and language. Sentences, utterances, and cognitive states are not representational *because* of their relations to inherently representational propositions. Instead, propositions are representational *because* of their relations to inherently representational cognitive states. Representation in mind and language results from the cognitive acts agents perform. One who sees an object o *as red* predicates redness of it. Since one's perceptual experience represents o as *being red*, one bears a propositional attitude to the proposition *that o is red*. Attitudes like this, as well as perceptual beliefs to which they give rise, are often not linguistically mediated.

The same is true of much, but not all, of our thought. Language learning changes our cognitive calculus by expanding our cognitive reach.[10] In making objects and properties with which we have had no prior acquaintance cognitively available to us, as well as providing the means of predicating one of the other, language vastly increases our stock of beliefs, and other attitudes. As a result, we come to bear attitudes to many propositions to which our only cognitive access is mediated by sentences that express

[8] Frege (1892b).
[9] This is Frege's problem "the concept horse is not a concept." See chapter 2 of Soames (2010).
[10] See Soames (1989).

them. Because of this, language is not merely a means of encoding and communicating prior, independent thought, but also a fertile source of new thought. Nevertheless, the explanatory model for understanding linguistic meaning applies to cognitive states generally, including perceptual cognitions, which lay the basis for more complex, linguistically mediated, thought.

I know of two ways of fleshing out a theory of propositions along these lines. On the *deflationary account*, propositions are theorists' constructs used to track predications, and other events, that make up our cognitive lives. On the *cognitive-realist account*, they are the very event-types instances of which deflationary propositions are used to track. Although neither has been fully developed, both are explored in Soames (2010). King (2007) presents a third important account, which, though differing in many particulars, shares with the views presented here the rejection of Frege-Russell propositions, and the use of agents' cognitive acts to explain the representational character of propositions. However, whereas King takes the crucial activities to involve agents' use of language, I take them to be acts that occur in all forms of cognition. In what follows, I limit my discussion to the deflationary and cognitive-realist approaches.[11]

5.231 THE DEFLATIONARY APPROACH

Deflationary propositions are structured complexes constructed out of, or encoding, the semantic contents of the constituents of sentences that express them. For illustration, I use a system of labeled bracketing to provide the structures. Whatever the right syntax for a language turns out to be, all semantically significant aspects of syntactic structure must be encoded by the deflationary propositions its sentences express. Presumably, if there is one system of semantic structures meeting this condition, there will be many. For any unambiguous sentence S, each such system identifies a unique structure as *the proposition S expresses*. However, since several systems may be equally good, several formal structures may be equally good candidates for being that proposition.

---

[11] For a discussion and critique of King (2007), see Soames (forthcoming c).

To entertain a simple proposition is to predicate something of something else. For example, to entertain the proposition *that o is red* is to predicate redness of o. Although, like negation, predication is a primitive notion, it is easily illustrated. When we see an object o *as red*, we predicate redness of it, and so entertain the proposition *that o is red*. We also predicate redness of o, and hence entertain this proposition, when we form the perceptual *belief* that o is red. We do the same when we understand an utterance of 'This is red', taking the predicate to express the property redness and the subject to refer to o.

The proposition entertained in these ways may be identified with (4).

4. $[_{Prop} [_{Arg} o] [_{Pred} Redness]]$

Structures like these are the theorist's creations. The theorist *stipulates* that to entertain (4) is to predicate redness of o, thereby assigning a new, technical meaning to the verb 'entertain' that explains what is meant by the theoretical claim that an agent entertains this structure. Next, the theorist advances (5a), which relates that claim to the ordinary claim on its left.

5a. An agent entertains the proposition that o is red iff the agent entertains (4).

A similar strategy is used for every propositional attitude. Since to entertain the proposition *that o is red* is to predicate redness of o, and since this predication is included in every attitude with that content, entertaining the proposition is one component of any attitude we bear to it. To *judge* that o is red is to predicate redness of o, while endorsing that predication. To *believe* that o is red is to be disposed to judge that o is red. To *know* that o is red is, roughly, to believe that o is red, while being justified in so doing in a case in which o *is* red. To *assert* that o is red is to make a conversational commitment, by assertively uttering something, to treat the proposition *that o is red* as something one knows. Given these characterizations, the theorist adds (5b–d) to (5a), thereby generating empirical predictions relating the theoretical claims on the right to ordinary attitude ascriptions on the left.

5b. An agent believes the proposition that o is red iff the agent believes (4).

   c. An agent knows that o is red iff the agent knows (4).

   d. An agent asserts that o is red iff the agent asserts (4).

More complex propositions are treated similarly. For example, to entertain the proposition *that it is not the case that o is red*, represented by (6), is (i) to predicate redness of o, and thereby to entertain (4), and (ii) to predicate *not being true* of (4), by, in effect, saying to oneself, "That's not true," referring to the result of one's initial predication.

6. $[_{\text{Prop}}[_{\text{Pred}} \text{ NEG}] \, [_{\text{Arg}} \, [_{\text{Prop}} \, [_{\text{Arg}} \, o] \, [_{\text{Pred}} \text{ Redness}]]]]$

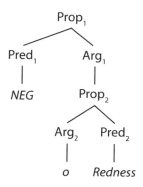

Entertaining other, more complex, propositions involves further, more complex, sequences of cognitive acts.

This approach depends on (i) the inclusion of information about what is predicated of what in abstract structures playing the role of propositions, (ii) the deflationary conception of what it is to bear cognitive attitudes to these structures, and (iii) their status as representational bearers of truth conditions in virtue of what is required to entertain them. What makes (4) represent o as red is that predicating its Pred-constituent of its Arg-constituent is necessary and sufficient for entertaining it. It is in virtue of this that we speak of (4) as predicating redness of o (whether or not anyone actually entertains it). Since a proposition that does this is true (at w) iff o is red (at w), the truth conditions of (4), which don't change from world-state to world-state, are derived from what it predicates of what.

On this approach, the function of propositions in our theories is to identify and track the cognitive states of agents. In physical theory we use numbers, and other abstract objects, to specify relations that physical magnitudes bear to one another. In semantic and cognitive theory we use abstract propositional structures to talk about the relations that representational cognitive states bear to one another, and to the world.[12] The conditions the theory specifies as necessary and sufficient for entertaining these structures are what allow us to use them to track the relations that hold among actual and possible predications by agents. This provides us with a sense in which the truth conditions of propositions are essential to them. What is essential to the use to which we put propositions is the range of actual and possible predications they track. Since these predications are essentially representational, that which tracks them is too.

Although one can get considerable mileage out of this approach, one may wonder whether propositions, regarded as merely useful tracking devices, are real objects of agents' attitudes. If the cognitive states being tracked are the only realities we are concerned with, such propositions may be nothing more than theoretically useful fictions. This is particularly worrying when one recalls that,

---

[12] This is the sense in which deflationary propositions are the theorist's own creations. To say this is not to say that the theorist creates the abstract structures used to track the predications of agents, but rather that this way of using them is his invention. For example, the deflationist is free to hold that for every rock r in the universe there is an abstract propositional structure paralleling (4) the terminal nodes of which are r and *being a rock*—even though no one (including the theorist) has every entertained it, or had any thoughts about r. A similar point holds for propositional structures involving properties that no one has ever predicated of anything (or ever will).

according to the theory, entertaining a compound structure like (6) requires agents first to refer to, and then to predicate untruth of, *the result of their predicating redness of o*—which is identified with the abstract structure (4). It is not clear how they can do this—come to have (4) in mind and use it to represent their predications—if the representational use of such structures is merely the invention of *the theorist*.

5.232 THE COGNITIVE-REALIST APPROACH

Since propositions are needed to track cognitive acts, why not take them to be *event-types* instances of which involve those very acts? On this proposal, the proposition *that o is red* is identified, not with the tree structure (4), but with the event-type in which an agent *predicates redness of o*. Thus, it is intrinsically connected to the cognitive acts it is needed to track. It is also something to which all agents who entertain it bear the same, natural, relation. Finally, this analysis gives us an account of what propositions *really are*, rather than merely choosing abstract structures, about which there is bound to be some arbitrariness, to *play the role of propositions*.[13]

Consider a spoken utterance of 'Snow is white', thought of as both an event that occurs at a particular time and place, and a token of the sentence uttered. So construed, sentences are event-types that can have multiple occurrences, which are their tokens.[14] Next imagine an utterance of the sentence followed by an utterance of "That's true." In such a case, the demonstrative may refer either to the utterance, or to the sentence uttered—illustrating that some event-types can be bearers of truth value. Finally, there

---

[13] The cognitive-realist approach (as well as the deflationary approach) was motivated, in part, by the desire to capture the central insight of Bertrand Russell's "multiple relation theory of judgment"—namely that talk of propositions is to be understood in terms of the cognitive activity of agents in predicating properties and relations of things, while avoiding the problems caused by Russell's attempt to do away with propositions. The connection to Russell is developed in chapter 4 of Soames (2010).

[14] The picture is complicated by the fact that some sentence tokens are utterances, while others are inscriptions. Perhaps sentence types should be understood disjunctively.

are events in which one doesn't utter anything, but simply thinks of snow as white, thereby predicating whiteness of it. These cognitions are events that occur at particular times and places, which are instances of the corresponding event-type in which an agent predicates whiteness of snow. Just as the sentence 'Snow is white' can be identified with the event-type of which utterances of it are instances, so *the proposition that snow is white* can be identified with the event-type of which particular cases of predicating whiteness of snow are instances. Thus, both event-types have truth conditions.

In addition to bearing their truth conditions intrinsically, propositions-*cum*-event-types are things with which we are acquainted. Since the proposition *that o is red* is the event-type in which one predicates redness of o, and since every attitude one bears to this proposition involves this predication, any agent acquainted with his own cognitive processes—in the sense of being able to make them objects of thought—will be similarly acquainted with the proposition *that o is red*, by virtue of being acquainted with events in his cognitive life that are instances of it (and noting their similarity). Given the means both of thinking of o as red, and of becoming aware of so doing, one can then make further predications about the content of one's thought. If, after one predicates redness of o, one says to oneself, "That's not true," one thereby predicates untruth of the proposition that is the type of cognitive event one has just brought about. This illustrates how agents are able to entertain compound propositions by predicating properties of their constituent propositions—which, as we saw, was the bane of the deflationary approach.

Thus, the cognitive-realist theory inherits the virtues of the deflationary theory, without its anti-realist worries. Like the deflationary account, it provides entities needed as contents of sentences, bearers of truth, and objects of the attitudes. But while the deflationary account sees nothing beyond the unavoidably arbitrary formal structures that play the role of propositions in our theories, the realist account views such structures as merely useful devices that *represent* the real propositions to which agents bear natural cognitive relations. The labeled trees provided by linguistic and cognitive theories encode the structure and sequence of cognitive acts that are necessary and sufficient for entertaining the real propositions these structures represent—where entertaining a proposition is performing the acts involved in tokening the event-type that it is.

Since performing those predicative acts involves representing certain things as being certain ways, we speak, derivatively, of the proposition itself as representing those things, and hence as being true or false, depending on whether the world is as it is represented to be. There are, of course, many propositions that have never been entertained—i.e., many cognitive event-types that haven't been tokened. But this is no more problematic than there being many sentences that have never been uttered. For a proposition to represent the world as being a certain way is for any *possible* predication that tokens it to do so. Whether or not there are actual tokens of this type makes no difference.

This account addresses the most vexing problems to which traditional propositions give rise. Unlike the Platonic epistemology traditionally required, the cognitive-realist account takes knowledge of propositions to be knowledge of events that make up one's cognitive life. It also avoids the pseudo-problem of "the unity of the proposition," which—though usually posed as that of explaining how the constituents of propositions "hold together"—serves to mask the real problem of explaining how propositions can be representational, and so have truth conditions. The traditional view makes this problem insoluble by taking the representational nature of propositions to be intrinsic, unanalyzable, and independent of us. By locating the representational character of propositions in their intrinsic connection to inherently representational cognitive events, the cognitive-realist account offers a solution.[15]

5.3 POSSIBLE WORLD-STATES

5.31 HOW TO UNDERSTAND POSSIBLE WORLD-STATES

Earlier I suggested that what commonly go by the name "possible worlds" are really possible world-states, which are properties attributed to the universe. Here I sketch a simple model for

---

[15] See chapters 6 and 7 of Soames (2010) for remaining challenges, and strategies for overcoming them.

understanding them, based on three leading ideas: (i) world-states are not alternate concrete worlds; they are properties specifying ways the world could be, or coherently be conceived to be (Stalnaker 1976); (ii) they need not be given purely qualitatively, but can be specified in terms of objects and properties (Kripke 1972); (iii) the space of world-states includes not only the actual and genuinely possible, but also the metaphysically impossible (Salmon 1989). The actual world-state is the maximal world-describing property that the world instantiates, metaphysically possible world-states are those that could have been instantiated, and epistemically possible states are those one cannot know apriori not to be instantiated.

Carnap's notion of *a state description* is the prototype for such properties. A Carnapian state-description is a complete, consistent set of atomic sentences or their negations (resulting in a complete assignment of truth values to atomic sentences). Truth values of complex sentences relative to a state description are determined using recursive rules for quantifiers, truth functions, and modal operators. In updating the picture, I replace Carnap's atomic sentences with structured propositions expressed by atomic formulas, relative to assignments of values to variables. Complete, consistent sets of such propositions, and their negations, are used to define world-states at which complex propositions are evaluated. Let D be a domain of objects, and B a set of properties expressed by simple predicates. A world-description S_w is a set each member of which is either an atomic proposition (an n-place property from B plus an n-tuple of objects from D) or the negation of such. S_w is complete iff for every atomic proposition, either it or its negation is a member of S_w. It is consistent iff its members can't be known apriori not to be jointly true. The world-state w corresponding to S_w is *the property of making the propositions in S_w true*. To conceive of w as instantiated is to conceive of every member of S_w being true, while taking the objects in the universe to include only those the existence of which is required by S_w. In addition, all apriori consequences of S_w are true at w.

All states in the structure are epistemically possible. The one that is instantiated is *actual*, those that could have been are *metaphysically possible*, and the rest are *metaphysically impossible*.

⌜Possibly/Necessarily S⌝ is true at w iff S is true at some/all world-states metaphysically possible from w. The truth values, at w, of propositions expressed by modal sentences are determined not by w itself, but by its position in the space of states. World-states metaphysically possible from one state may differ from those possible from another. For each epistemically possible state w_1, there are states w_2 that would be metaphysically possible, if w_1 were instantiated. These are properties the universe could have had, if it had had w_1. For each such w_2 there are states w_3 that would be metaphysically possible, if w_2 were instantiated. These are properties that it could have been the case that, the universe could have had, if it had had w_1. A world-state w is a property that gives a complete story of what the universe would be like if w were instantiated. Since it is no part of that story to specify what the universe would be like if other world-states were instantiated, the propositions defining w don't contain explicit information about other states. Nevertheless, for any proposition p and world-state w^*, we can evaluate the proposition *that p is true at w^** at any world-state. We need only remember that a proposition can be true at a world-state without being one of the propositions that define it.

This model works well in giving semantics for simple first-order modal languages. More complex world-states are needed for evaluating more complex languages. For example, if causal statements—⌜A's F-ing caused B's G-ing⌝—and/or propositional attitude ascriptions—⌜A believes that S⌝—are included, then world-state-constituting sets must contain sufficiently many propositions expressed by such sentences to determine a complete world-story—i.e., one that answers every question. I follow Stalnaker (1981b) in taking this to mean *every question relevant to the inquiry at hand*. When world-states are attributed to the universe, they are taken to capture everything relevant to a given inquiry. However, for every inquiry that might be undertaken, there may be another for which a more fine-grained, fully-articulated space of states would be needed—in which case, there will be no absolute sense in which world-states encode maximally informative stories about the universe that evaluate every conceivable proposition. Instead, they are properties *treated as maximal* for specific purposes. The properties are there independently. It is the use to which we put them that is relative to us.

5.32 *The Relationship between Modal and Nonmodal Truths*

World-states are properties of making world-describing sets S_w of basic nonmodal propositions true. S_w must be *consistent*, in the sense that its members can't be known apriori not to be jointly true, as well as *maximal*, in the sense of providing answers to all relevant questions. In addition to members of S_w, the propositions *true at w* include (i) truth-functional compounds and quantified propositions that are apriori consequences of S_w (plus the assumption that the existing individuals are those required by S_w), and (ii) modal propositions, the truth of which is determined by the propositions true at world-states possible from w. Although S_w is free of modal propositions, typically it will contain propositions— e.g., *that I am human* and *that I am the father of Greg and Brian Soames*—which have modal consequences that constrain which world-states are metaphysically possible from w. The degree to which the modal truths at w may float free of the nonmodal truths is controversial. On one point, however, the model takes a stand. In excluding modal propositions from S_w, it presupposes that world-states that agree on all nonmodal truths are identical; hence those that support different modal truths must differ in their nonmodal truths. Although this presupposition is plausible, it could be rejected, in which case modal propositions would sometimes have to be included in world-state defining sets.

5.33 *Our Knowledge of World-States*

Since world-states are properties of making sets S_w of basic propositions true, knowledge of world-states is often apriori knowledge of propositions. When p is an apriori consequence of S_w (plus the assumption that the existing objects are those required by S_w), the proposition *that p is true at w* can be known apriori. This is true at the actual world-state @ iff someone knows apriori *that p is true at w*, at some world-state possible from @. The point generalizes to world-states w* distinct from @.

The ease with which knowledge of the truth values of propositions at other world-states can, in principle, be had is an attractive feature of the model. However, it may also seem to be in tension with another attractive feature—the exclusion from S_w of ascriptions of truth values to propositions at other world-states. The reason for the exclusion was obvious. World-states are properties incorporating complete stories of what the world would be like if they were instantiated. Since what the world would be like if w^* were instantiated is no part of the story of what the world would be like if w were instantiated, *that p is true/false at w^** shouldn't be a member of S_w. This doesn't mean that such world-state-indexed propositions can't be true at w. On the contrary. If p is true at w^*, then *that p is true at w^** is true at every world-state.

Now for the potential conflict. When agents at w have beliefs, S_w will include belief ascriptions. Since the truth, at w, of (7) requires only the truth of p at w^*, the truth, at w of (8) doesn't require (7) to be a member of S_w.

7. p is true at w^*.
8. A believes truly that p is true at w^*.

What about (9)—which we may take to be true at w?

9. A knows that p is true at w^*.

If (9) is apriori calculable from (8), plus members of S_w specifying the justification of A's belief, the reliability of A's cognitive processes, etc., then S_w needn't include (7). Thus, the truth of (9) at w requires no modification of the model, if—whenever 'S' in (10) is replaced by a sentence expressing a proposition that A knows at w—(10) is an apriori consequence of the propositions about belief, reliability, etc. used to define w.

10. If S, then A knows that S.

However, if these instances of (10) aren't apriori consequences of those propositions, S_w may have to include (9). Since (7) is an apriori consequence of (9), the story of what the world would be like if w were instantiated *would* then entail a partial account of what the world would be like if w^* were instantiated. However, this isn't really problematic. Since (7) is itself apriori, it is an apriori consequence of the empty set of propositions. So, there is still no rationale for including it in S_w.[16]

5.34 Existent and Nonexistent World-States

Possible world-states are complex properties, the constituents of which are individuals and properties. Since the existence of complex, uninstantiated properties doesn't, in general, cause problems, the existence of uninstantiated world-states doesn't either—if their constituents exist. This suggests that some merely possible world-states actually exist. Still, certain modal truths seem to be about merely possible individuals. One such truth is (11a), which, according to possible worlds semantics, is true only if (11b) is.

11a. It could have been the case that I had a sister.
  b. At some world-state w possible from @, there is an individual who is my sister.

This is troubling. Although I could have had a sister, no actually existing individual could have been my sister. Since *possible world-states at which I have a sister* are complex properties one of the constituents of which doesn't (actually) exist, it would seem that such states don't exist either (even though they could have). How, then, can (11a) be true?

It is true because the *some world-state* quantifier in (11b) ranges over both world-states that exist and those that don't. Although this is controversial, the idea that we can refer to, and quantify over, only things that exist is, I believe, an unfounded philosophical prejudice at variance with our ordinary thought and talk. For instance, imagine that I have all the materials to build a doghouse, plus a plan specifying every detail of the design and construction, including how each of the materials will be used. From studying the plan and materials, I know exactly which structure I intend to create. Having identified it uniquely, I can refer to it, predicate properties of it, and even name it. After I do, I can truly say "Although Yasnaya Polyana doesn't exist yet, it soon will, and tomorrow Lassie will move into it." Since this remark is true, I must now be able to refer to the object, and truly predicate properties of it, even though it

[16] See Soames (2007a) for potential complications.

doesn't yet exist. And if I can do that, I can also quantify over it, by saying "The name 'Yasnaya Polyana' refers to something I plan to build." So, nonexistence is no bar to quantification.

This example involves reference to, and quantification over, something that doesn't exist, but will. Nothing of significance changes if the object never exists because I don't carry out the plan, even though I could. In such a case, the fact that Yasnaya Polyana's existence is merely possible doesn't prevent me from referring to, naming, or quantifying over it—by saying "The name 'Yasnaya Polyana' refers to something I could have constructed, but didn't."[17] For more far-reaching cases see Salmon (1987). Since world-states are complex properties the constituents of which are individuals and properties, the same conclusions drawn about nonexistent, but possible, objects apply to nonexistent possible world-states.[18] Since reference to an entity requires one to identify it uniquely, whereas quantification over it doesn't, reference to possible but nonexistent objects, properties, and world-states is harder than quantification over them. Because we are in no position to identify many merely possible objects, and many possible, but nonexistent, world-states, we can't name or directly refer to them. However, this doesn't prevent us from quantifying over them, which is all that possible worlds semantics requires.

5.35 *The Function of World-States in Our Theories*

In this discussion, I have used the term "possible worlds semantics" to refer to theories that state the truth conditions of sentences containing modal expressions like 'could', 'would', and 'possibly' in terms of related claims about world-states. Although both the theories and the term are standard, the word 'semantics'

---

[17] Nonexistence is also no bar to having properties. In the above examples, Yasnaya Polyana has the properties *being something I will build,* or *could have built,* even though it doesn't (actually) exist. If one were worried about the existence conditions of propositions, one could extend the point to them by holding that they can *be true,* or *false,* at w even if they don't exist at w. However, this raises the issue of the existence conditions of event-types, which I here leave open.

[18] The point extends to possibly possible objects, properties, and world-states, possibly possibly possible examples, and so on.

has suggested to many (i) that the *meanings* of sentences containing ordinary modal expressions are given by the possible-world specifications of their truth conditions, and (ii) that our ordinary modal notions are *analyzable* in terms of possible world-states. These are mistakes.

Even if (i) were true, (ii) wouldn't be. Since metaphysically possible world-states are world-describing properties the universe *could* have instantiated, conceptual priority belongs to our ordinary modal notions, rather than the other way around. As for (i), replacing worlds with world-states, and allowing quantification over the merely possible, make the commitments of "possible worlds semantics" far more plausible than they would otherwise be. So understood, such theories are quite defensible. However, the defensibility of a philosophical theory doesn't justify reading it into the meanings of sentences used by ordinary speakers, and the commitments they undertake in accepting them. Possible world-states are useful tools for regimenting modal reasoning, investigating modal claims, and formulating systematic theories of the truth conditions of modal sentences and propositions. But this doesn't show that ordinary modal sentences make explicit claims about world-states, or that understanding them requires one to have the concept of such a state.

Selected Further Reading

Frege, Gottlob (1892a), "On Sense and Reference."
——— (1892b), "On Concept and Object."
——— (1918), "The Thought."
King, Jeffrey C. (2007), *The Nature and Structure of Content.*
Lewis, David (2001), *The Plurality of Worlds.*
Rosen, Gideon (1990), "Modal Fictionalism."
Russell, Bertrand (1903), *Principles of Mathematics.*
Salmon, Nathan (1987), "Existence."
——— (1989), "On the Logic of What Might Have Been."
Soames, Scott (2007a), "Actually."
——— (2010), *What Is Meaning?*
Stalnaker, Robert (1976), "Possible Worlds."
——— (1984), *Inquiry.*

Apriority, Aposteriority, and Actuality

6.1 LANGUAGE, PHILOSOPHY, AND THE MODALITIES

Much philosophical reasoning consists in tracing "modal connections" among sentences and propositions, and drawing conclusions from, or about, them. The connections are truth guarantees in which, for various senses of 'must', one set of sentences or propositions *must be true* if other sets of sentences or propositions are. When such a relation holds between two sets, the former is a *consequence* of the latter. If a set is a consequence of the empty set, its members *must be true*, without qualification. When the bearers are sentences, the relevant modalities are *logical* and *analytic* truth, and consequence. When they are propositions, the relevant modalities are *apriori* and *necessary* truth, and consequence, plus *counterfactual* consequence. We owe the conception of logical truth as truth in all models mainly to Tarski, the conception of analytic truth as one that can be reduced to logical truths by putting synonyms for synonyms mainly to Frege, and the conception of counterfactual consequence as truth in all "closest" world-states in which the initial set is true mainly to Stalnaker and Lewis. We owe the identification of metaphysical necessity, and the clear distinction between necessity and apriority, mainly to Kripke. These advances, sketched in earlier chapters, have changed the face of philosophy. Here, I attempt to extend those lessons, by combining the earlier discussions of rigid designation, direct reference, and indexicality with chapter 5's account of world-states.

6.2 Apriority and Actuality

6.21 *Apriori Knowledge of the Truth of Aposteriori Propositions at the Actual World-State*

Since a world-state w is a maximally informative set S_w of world-describing propositions, and since, by definition, the propositions true at w include all apriori consequences of S_w, the proposition *that p is true at w* is knowable apriori whenever p is an apriori consequence of S_w.[1] It is also true at every world-state, and hence necessary, even if p is contingent. Since it is normal for apriori truths to be necessary, and vice versa, this isn't surprising. However, the resulting puzzle about the actual world-state @ is. When p is an apriori consequence of $S_@$, the proposition *that p is true at @* is knowable apriori, even when p is contingent and knowable only aposteriori. But surely, it may be objected, p and the claim *that p is true at the actual world-state* are equivalent. Since each is an apriori consequence of the other, one who knows the latter apriori can come to know the former apriori by deriving it from what he already knows. But now we have a contradiction.

Although something has gone wrong, it is not thesis (1), which tacitly relies on A1–A3.

1. For all world-states *w*, and propositions p that are apriori consequences of S_w, the proposition *that p is true at w* is knowable apriori.
A1. To say that p is true at w is just to say that p would be true if w were instantiated.
A2. If it is knowable apriori that p is true if $q_1 \ldots q_n$ are (i.e., if p is an apriori consequence of $q_1 \ldots q_n$), then it is knowable apriori that p would be true if *the property of making $q_1 \ldots q_n$ true* were instantiated.
A3. If w = *the property of making $q_1 \ldots q_n$ true*, then it is knowable apriori that p would be true if w were instan-

---

[1] A proposition p is knowable apriori iff there is some way of entertaining p such that, when one does so, it is possible to come to know p, without appeal to empirical evidence for justification.

tiated, if it is knowable apriori that p would be true if *the property of making $q_1 \ldots q_n$ true* were instantiated.

A1 merely specifies what 'p is true at w' means, and so is unproblematic, as is A2. Given our account of world-states, one can deny (1) only by denying A3. This is not possible, if its italicized phrase α is treated not as a description (which it isn't), but as a directly referential term substitutable for 'w'. The same is true, if knowing the proposition expressed by a sentence '... α ...' is sufficient to (be in position to) know *de re*, the proposition expressed by '... w ...' (though perhaps not vice versa). Since this requirement is met, (1) must be accepted.[2]

The other thesis used to generate the contradiction was (2), the basis for which was (3).

2. For all propositions p, the proposition *that p is true at @* is apriori equivalent to p.

3. For all propositions p, the proposition *that p is true at the actual world-state* is apriori equivalent to p.

Although (2) and (3) appear similar, they are logically different. The truth of (1) depends on the apriority of every proposition expressed by

1a. the proposition *that p is true at w*

relative to an assignment of a world-state to 'w', and of a proposition to 'p' that is an apriori consequence of the set of propositions

---

[2] 'The property *being ...*' and ⌜the propery of making the proposition that $S_1 \ldots$ the proposition that S_n true⌝ (which is how italicized phrase in A3 may be understood) are *articulated terms* in the sense of Richard (1993). Although such terms have some features of directly referential terms, they may not always be substitutable for coreferential Millian terms without changing the proposition expressed. Soames (forthcoming b) shows why, even so, truth-preserving substitution works in one direction: knowing the proposition expressed by a sentence containing an articulated term is sufficient for knowing the proposition expressed by the corresponding sentence containing a coreferential Millian term—which is all that is required by A3.

defining the world-state assigned to 'w'. Since the semantic content of a variable, at an assignment, is simply the entity so assigned, the proposition expressed by (1a) relative to an assignment of @ to 'w' is a bare, Russellian proposition that predicates *being true at* of the proposition and that state—independent of any particular way of apprehending the pair. This proposition *is* both necessary and knowable apriori, as is the proposition expressed by (1b), if '@' names the actual world-state, and, names are Millian.

> 1b. the proposition *that p is true at* @

By contrast, the proposition expressed by (1c), in which a *non-rigid description* designates @, is contingent and knowable only aposteriori (when the one expressed by 'p' is).

> 1c. the proposition that p is true at *the world-state that is actual* (i.e., that obtains or is instantiated)

If 'the actual world-state', in (3), is understood as equivalent to the nonrigid description in (1c), then (3) is true—since anyone who accepts S is justified in accepting ⌜It is true that S at the world-state that is actual⌝, and vice versa. However, this tells us nothing about (2), which is understood quite differently. To assess it, we need to bring in indexical reference to @.

6.22 *The Contingent Apriori and the Apriori Equivalence of P and the Proposition* That P Is True at @

Consider again the indexical operator 'actually', discussed in 4.32–4.34. Since its content at context C is the property *being true at* w_C, uses of ⌜Actually S⌝ at @ express the proposition *that p is true at* @ (where p is expressed by S). This proposition is both necessary and knowable apriori whenever p is true. It is also apriori equivalent to p, as is shown by the fact that one who, at @, knows the apriori truth expressed by (4a) can derive the proposition expressed by (4e), by steps that can be known apriori to be truth-preserving.

> 4a. S iff S.
> b. So, it is true at this very world-state (said demonstrating @) that *S iff S*.

   c. So, it is true at this very world-state (said demonstrating @) that *S iff it is true at this very world-state* (said demonstrating @) *that S.*

   d. So, S iff it is true at this very world-state (said demonstrating @) that S.

   e. So, S iff actually S.

The move to (4b) is justified, since for any proposition p, if at w, A knows p, then A needs no further justification to come to know, of w, that it is a world-state at which p is true. Thus, apriori knowledge of proposition (4a) is sufficient for apriori knowledge, of @, that it is a world-state at which proposition (4a) is true. But if one knows, of *this very state*, @, that it makes that proposition true, then one needs no further information to draw the same conclusion about the proposition expressed by ⌜S iff it is true at *this very state* that S⌝. So, proposition (4c) is knowable apriori. Now note: if a use, at w, of ⌜It is true at this very world-state that R⌝ (said demonstrating w) expresses knowledge based on evidence E (where E may be null), then a corresponding use of R does too. Thus, the apriority of (4c) guarantees the apriority of proposition (4d)/(4e). Hence, (2) is true—the proposition *that p is true at @* is apriori equivalent to p, even if p is both contingent and knowable only aposteriori, and the proposition *that p is true at @* is both necessary and knowable apriori. In such cases, (4e) is an instance of the contingent apriori.

6.23 *Why Apriority Isn't Closed under Apriori Consequence: Two Ways of Knowing @*

The solution to our puzzle is nearly at hand. (1), (2), and (5) entail a contradiction.

   5. All apriori consequences of propositions that are knowable apriori are themselves knowable apriori.

Let p be a contingent truth that is knowable only aposteriori. It follows from (1) that the proposition *that p is true at @* is knowable apriori. It follows from (2) that these two propositions are apriori consequences of one another. Adding (5) yields the conclusion that p *is* knowable apriori. Since this contradicts our choice of p as aposteriori, the truth of (1) and (2) shows (5) to be false. How it can be?

How can the contingent aposteriori p, which *is* an apriori consequence of the apriori truth *that p is true at @*, not be knowable apriori? The reason is that the epistemic route to p from its apriori counterpart is different from, and at odds with, the route to the apriority of the latter. For p to be derivable from *that p is true at @*, @ must be given as *this very world-state* (the one that obtains). However, to know apriori *that p is true at @*, one must be given the propositions that define @. *That p is true at @* is entertainable in two radically different ways. One way involves grasping the propositional content of @. One who entertains the proposition in this way can know it apriori, by deriving p from propositions defining @. But this way of presenting @ provides no way of knowing that it is instantiated. Hence, when the proposition *that p is true at @* is entertained in a way that allows one to know it apriori, one can't infer p from it. The second, indexical, way of entertaining the proposition *that p is true at @*—which is how it is presented using the actuality operator—doesn't involve grasping the (full) propositional content of @. When presented with the proposition in this way, one can't determine its truth apriori, though one can move apriori from it to p, and vice versa. Since neither way of knowing *that p is true at @* allows one to establish p apriori, p is knowable only aposteriori.

6.24 *Apriori Truths That Are Known Only Aposteriori*

Returning to our starting point, we reaffirm that for all world-states w, it is knowable apriori *that p is true at w*, whenever p is an apriori consequence of S_w. Accepting this, one might still object that since the size and complexity of the set $S_@$ will always exceed our cognitive limitations, as a practical matter we will never grasp the content of @, and so will never *know* apriori *that p is true at @*. Thus, the objector maintains, the sense in which any such proposition is *knowable* apriori is, at best, an attenuated one. This is wrong on two counts.

First, it ignores the point made in 5.31, that since the space and constitution of world-states are inquiry-relative, what counts as "the actual world-state" depends on the inquiry at hand. To be sure, there are many complex inquiries for which the space of relevant possibilities is vast, and the individual states, including the one that obtains, are too complex for us to cognitively entertain. In such cases, truths expressed by ⌜p is true at @⌝ will, if known by us, be known only aposteriori—despite being *knowable* apriori. However, this is not so for other, more limited, inquiries. When the question is how a departmental vote, or tonight's Yankee game, will turn out, both the space of world-states and their complexity may be entertainable by agents with our cognitive capacities. In such cases nothing prevents us from coming to know the proposition expressed by ⌜p is true at @⌝ apriori, even if we happen to know it only aposteriori.

The second way in which the objection goes wrong concerns inquiries for which the space of world-states is vast, and the individual states are too complex for us to entertain (nonindexically). In these cases, truths expressed by ⌜p is true at @⌝ are, in principle, knowable apriori, even though our cognitive limitations prevent us from knowing them in that way. However, this does not, as the objection maintains, show that they are apriori in only an attenuated sense. The fact that their contents exceed our cognitive limitations doesn't distinguish them from many apriori truths of logic and mathematics that are too complex for us to entertain, even though they are expressed by theorems of correct logical or mathematical theories. We don't deny that these propositions are knowable apriori in the standard sense, even though our cognitive limitations afford us no way of knowing them, short of using aposteriori methods (like running a reliable computer for a long time). The point is the same for propositions expressed by uses of ⌜p is true at @⌝ or ⌜Actually S⌝—save for the fact, that, in addition to being knowable apriori, the way in which they are known aposteriori, when @ is presented indexically, is one we rely on all the time.

6.25 *Apriority and Epistemic Possibility*

Since necessary truths are those true at all metaphysically possible world-states, it may seem that apriori truths are those true at all epistemically possible states. But this is only half right. Any proposition true at all epistemically possible states is knowable

137

apriori, but not vice versa. For every contingent truth p, the proposition *that p is true iff p is true at* @ is contingent, but knowable apriori. Hence, there is a metaphysically possible world-state at which it is false. Since this world-state could have been instantiated, imagining it to be can't be incoherent. So it is epistemically possible. Thus, a proposition can be knowable apriori, even if it isn't true at all epistemically possible states.

The temptation to think otherwise comes from the temptation to accept (6).

6. If it can be known apriori both (i) that p is false, and (ii) that p is true at w, then it can be known apriori (iii) that w is not instantiated.

The falsity of (6) is illustrated by (7).

7a. Plato was a philosopher iff actually (i.e., it is true at @ that) Plato was a philosopher.

b. ~ Plato was a philosopher & actually (i.e., it is true at @ that) Plato was a philosopher.

Plato was, contingently, a philosopher; so there is a metaphysically possible world-state w at which the proposition *expressed at* @ by (7a) is false, and the proposition expressed by (7b) is true. Since w and the world-states surrounding it are properties of making sets of basic world-describing propositions true, they can be identified in terms of those propositions.

P1.   the proposition that Plato was a philosopher
P2.   the proposition that Plato lived in Athens

A Simplified Space of World-States

@	w	w*	w#
P1	~P1	P1	~P1
P2	P2	~P2	~P2

Here we pretend that complete world-stories can be told in terms of P1 and P2. In a more realistic example, the number of propositions would be greater, and the world-state-defining sets larger, and more numerous. However, this doesn't affect our result, as long as these sets don't ascribe truth values to propositions at other world-states. Given this, we can reduce the question *Can the world-state w, in which (7b) is true, be known apriori not to be instantiated?* to the question *Can it be known apriori that ~P1 and P2 aren't jointly true?* Since this can't be known apriori, it can't be known apriori that w isn't instantiated. So, the consequent of (6) is false.

The falsity of (6) follows from the apriority of the claims (i) *that p is false*, and (ii) *that p is true at w*—where p is the proposition (expressed at @ by) (7b). Since the corresponding proposition (7a) is knowable apriori, and anyone who knows it can infer that (7b) is false, (i) is knowable apriori. Thus, (6) is false iff (ii)—which amounts to (8)—is knowable apriori.

> 8. If ~P1 and P2 were true, then ~P1 and *that P1 is true at @* would also be true.

This is knowable apriori if it is knowable apriori *that P1 is true at @*. But, when the truth of q is calculable from the propositions defining w, it is always knowable apriori that q is true at w. Thus, (8) is knowable apriori, and (6) is false.[3]

The falsity of (6) is another example of the failure of apriority to be closed under apriori consequence. Here, one proposition— (i) of (6)—can be known apriori only when @ is presented indexically—as it is in "It is false that (~ Plato was a philosopher & actually Plato was a philosopher)"—while another proposition— (ii) of (6)—can be known apriori only when it is known apriori that Plato was a philosopher at @, which requires @ to be presented in terms of its propositional content. Since there is no way of merging the apriori routes to (i) and (ii) into a single route to (iii), one can't derive (iii) from apriori knowledge of (i) and (ii).

So, propositions expressed by ⌜S iff actually S⌝ are genuine examples of the contingent apriori, and the world-states at which they are false are epistemically, as well as metaphysically, possible.

---

[3] Contrary to the suggestion on p. 296 of (reprinted) Soames (2007a), the same result holds even if *that A knows (7b*)* is added to the world-defining propositions for w—if we observe the distinction between simple and articulated terms for @ mentioned in the previous note and form (7b*) using an articulated term for @ instead of the Millian term '@' used in (7b).

The reason that knowing these propositions at @ doesn't require empirical evidence to rule out these states is that indexical reference to the very world-state at which they are known renders other states irrelevant.

6.26 *Are Singular Thoughts Instances of the Contingent Apriori?*

There is another putative route to the contingent apriori, due to Kripke and Kaplan, about which I am skeptical. Let D be a nonrigid definite description, and n be a new proper name introduced with the stipulation that its bearer is to be whatever D denotes. Then, (9a) is necessary, but (9b) and (9c) are contingent, since names and 'dthat'-descriptions are rigid.

9a.   If D exists, the D is D.
  b.   If n exists, then n is D.
  c.   If dthat D exists, then dthat D is D.

Since no information beyond that required to understand them is needed to determine their truth, it is further claimed that each expresses a proposition that is knowable apriori. However, as argued in Donnellan (1977) and Salmon (1988), knowing that the sentences (9b) and (9c) express true propositions is one thing, while knowing the true propositions they express is another. Thus, the argument is inconclusive.

Recognizing some merit in this critique, Kripke has said that he never meant to suggest that one could introduce a name using *any description*, and use it to generate belief in, or knowledge of, singular propositions about its referent. Let F be an arbitrary falsehood that A believes to be true, and N be a name introduced by stipulating that its bearer is to be whatever satisfies ⌜the x: if F, then x = Princeton University, but if ~F, x = Plato⌝. A will then understand (10), and believe it to be true, even though N designates someone A knows not to be a university.

10. N is a university.

Since one should not, Kripke thinks, attribute to A the belief that Plato is a university, he recognizes that one can't, in general, establish (11c) by deriving it from (11a) and (11b), when A has stipulated that n is to designate whatever D denotes.[4]

11a. A believes/knows that ... D ...
  b. A understands and believes/knows the sentence '. . . n . . .' to be true
  c. A believes/knows that ... n ...

So why did Kripke think names introduced by descriptions could be used to generate instances of the contingent apriori? The cases he had in mind, he says, are those in which we introduce a name using a description the denotation of which we are already acquainted with.[5] To test this, imagine my seeing a man m standing in front of me, and thinking, "He is standing in front of me." My knowledge, of m, that he is standing in front of me is based on, and justified by, my perceptual experience. Hence it is aposteriori. This wouldn't change if I were to introduce the name 'Saul' stipulating that it is to refer to *the man standing in front of me*. If I were to do so, 'Saul is standing in front of me' would express the aposteriori proposition I already knew. The same is true of the weaker proposition I express by saying 'He is the man standing in front of me, *if anyone is*', in a situation in which I see m, and believe him to be standing in front of me, but don't feel sure that anyone is really there because I harbor (unfounded) doubts about perceptual illusions. Still, my knowledge that if anyone is standing in front of me, he, m, is standing there is aposteriori. In addition to being based on the perceptual experience that allows me to entertain this proposition, my knowledge is *justified* by the experience. Hence, the knowledge I express by saying "If anyone is standing in front of me, then he [demonstrating m] is standing in front of me" is aposteriori, as is the knowledge expressed by saying "If anyone is standing in front of me, then Saul is standing in front of me"—after I have introduced 'Saul' to stand for the man, if any, who is standing in front of me.

---

[4] For discussion, see chapter 16 of Soames (2003b).
[5] See Salmon (1988), p. 200.

For reasons like this, I am skeptical that names introduced by descriptions—and 'dthat'-rigidified descriptions—are ever sources of the contingent apriori. However, this view is controversial. The general relationship between descriptive vs. singular (*de re*) thought remains incompletely understood, and the subject of intense investigation along several interesting lines. My perspective is developed a little further in Soames (forthcoming a). More liberal conceptions of the relationship between the two can be found in Sosa (1970), Harman (1977), Jeshion (2001), and Hawthorne and Manley (forthcoming).

6.3 'Actually'

The actuality operator used above is a valuable tool. But does it capture the ordinary meaning of 'actually'? Initially, there appears to be evidence on both sides. On the positive side, (12) is evidence that 'actually' can function as a rigidifier.

12. It could have been the case, had just a few things gone differently, that the person who actually won the election wasn't elected at all.

What I say in uttering (12) is true iff the one who won the election at @ lost it at a world-state differing minimally from @. This is expected, if *actually* is a rigidifier. On the negative side, uttering (13a) seems to differ from uttering (13b) only in signaling that the information asserted may be unexpected, which seems to suggest that S and ⌜Actually S⌝ differ only rhetorically.

13a. Actually, I live in California.
  b. I live in California.

Although these observations seem to point in opposite directions, they really don't. The all-too-ubiquitous rhetorical use of 'actually' is compatible with its analysis as an indexical referring to @. This reference is responsible for its rigidifying effect on descriptions, and for the necessity of ⌜Actually S⌝ when S is contingent. The indexicality of 'actually' allows us routinely to pass back and forth between S and ⌜Actually S⌝, even though the propositions they express differ dramatically. Because of this effortless inferential interchange, an assertive utterance of either sentence standardly results in the assertion of the propositions expressed by both.

This assertive equivalence can be used to explain the rhetorical effect of 'actually' in examples like (13a). Since adding it to S doesn't change what is asserted, one who does so is presumed to have a nonassertive reason for referring to @, and explicitly saying that the proposition p (expressed by S) is true *at* @, rather than simply asserting p by uttering S. Often, the reason is to contrast @ with other states one's hearers find salient, or expect to be instantiated. I may utter (13a) to someone who imagines me (still) living in Princeton. By calling attention to @, and explicitly saying that *at* @, I live in California, I contrast @ with possible states at which I live elsewhere. Thus, the indexical semantics that gives 'actually' its logical punch also is capable of explaining its rhetorical use in (13a).

However, not all uses of 'actually' in English fit this model so well. We can easily imagine uses of (14) in which what is intended can't be captured by taking 'actually' to be the indexical operator of philosophical semantics, unless that operator takes wide-scope over the entire counterfactual.

14. If the richer of the two candidates had won, instead of losing, as he in fact did, my electoral formula would actually have made the correct prediction.

This suggests that further work on the use of 'actually' in English is needed.

Selected Further Reading

Hawthorne, John, and David Manley (forthcoming), *The Reference Book*.

Jeshion, Robin (2001), "Acquaintanceless *De Re* Belief."

Kaplan, David (1989a), "Demonstratives."

Kripke, Saul (1972), *Naming and Necessity*.

Salmon, Nathan (1988), "How to Measure the Standard Metre."

Soames, Scott (2003b), *Philosophical Analysis in the Twentieth Century,* vol. 2: *The Age of Meaning,* chapter 16.

—— (2007a), "Actually."

—— (forthcoming a), "Kripke on Epistemic and Metaphysical Possibility: Two Routes to the Necessary Aposteriori."

The Limits of Meaning

7.1 THE TRADITIONAL CONCEPTION OF MEANING, THOUGHT, ASSERTION, AND IMPLICATURE

On the traditional view, the meaning of a nonindexical (declarative) sentence is the proposition it expresses, while the meaning of a sentence containing an indexical, or other context-sensitive expression, is a rule for determining the different propositions it expresses in different contexts of utterance. In short, the meaning of S is a function from contexts C to propositions expressed by S in C—where, if S is nonindexical, the function yields the same proposition for every C. This proposition is often described as what S "says" in C. Although it is really speakers, not sentences, that *say* things, this informal terminology is justified by the close connection traditionally seen between the semantic content of S in C and the proposition asserted by a speaker who utters S in C. Special cases aside, such a speaker is taken to assert the proposition S semantically expresses, plus some of its most obvious consequences (such as the conjuncts of a conjunction). This is the core, but not the whole, of the information carried by the utterance.

In addition to asserting propositions, utterances also carry *conversational implicatures,* in the sense of Grice (1967), which arise not from the meanings of the sentences uttered, but from the communicative uses to which they are put. For Grice, the chief goal of most communication is the cooperative exchange of information, which is governed by conversational maxims for securing its efficient achievement. The combined force of these maxims directs one to make a maximally informative, succinct, and relevant contribution (given the aims of the conversation) for which one has adequate evidence. A *conversational implicature* is a proposition, over and above what one asserts, belief in which is required by the presumption that one is obeying the maxims. In standard cases, a speaker s conversationally implicates q by saying p iff (i) s is presumed to be obeying the maxims, (ii) the supposition that s believes q is required to make s's saying p consistent with this presumption, and (iii) s thinks that s's hearers recognize both the requirement reported in (ii) and that s knows that they recognize the requirement.[1]

Well-known examples include (i) the case of the professor, who, when asked for a job recommendation, writes only that her student speaks good English and attends class regularly, thereby implicating that there is nothing good to say about his ability to teach philosophy, and (ii) the case of one who, when addressed by a stranded motorist seeking help who says "I'm out of gas," responds "There is a gas station around the corner," thereby implicating that it is, or may be, open for business. More philosophically significant examples include (iii) the implicature that one who asserts a disjunction has non-truth-functional grounds for believing it (refuting a suggestion that the logician's 'or' differs from the ordinary 'or'), (iv) the implicature that one who says ⌜It's true that S⌝ (rather than simply S) is referring to a previously made, or contemplated, remark, and conceding or endorsing it (refuting Strawson's performative analysis of truth), and (v) the related implicature that one who says ⌜Actually S⌝ (rather than simply S) is contrasting the actual world-state with salient possible states at which S is untrue.[2] In each case, the conversational

---

[1] As Jeff King has reminded me, Grice's own characterization allows some cases in which one conversationally implicates q in which one doesn't say (assert) p, but only "makes as if to say (assert) p." He has in mind instances of irony, like those in which one utters "He's a fine friend" in a situation that makes it clear that one's intention is to convey the opposite. The issue is whether the speaker has literally asserted (among other things) that the man is a fine friend as part of an effort to communicate something else, or whether the fact that the speaker isn't, in the end, committed to the truth of the proposition literally expressed by the use of the sentence means that he shouldn't really be regarded as asserting it, but only as "making as if to assert it." Although I incline, with Grice, to the latter alternative, I here bypass these technicalities in favor of the simpler formulation, which will serve our purposes. For more, see Grice (1967) and Soames (2008c).

[2] See Grice (1967), plus chapters 5 and 9 of Soames (2003b).

implicature is not asserted, but merely conveyed by the fact that the speaker said what he/she did.

Grice also identifies what he calls *conventional implicatures*, which are non-asserted suggestions generated by non-truth-conditional aspects of the meaning of the sentence uttered. For example, an utterance of 'She is poor but honest' implicates (due to the meaning of 'but') that there is a contrast between poverty and honesty; an utterance of 'He is an Englishman, and therefore, brave' implicates (due to the meaning of 'therefore') that being brave is usual for Englishmen; and an utterance of 'Ed hasn't arrived yet' implicates (due to the meaning of 'yet') that Ed's arrival is expected.[3] These suggestions, along with what an utterance asserts, and conversationally implicates, make up the bulk of the information it carries, on the traditional picture.[4] The relationship between semantic content and assertion is given in (1).

1. One who assertively utters S (speaking literally, and without conversational implicatures canceling the normal force of the remark) in a context C says, or asserts, *the semantic content of S in C*, also known as *the proposition semantically expressed by S in C*. Any additional propositions asserted are obvious and relevant consequences of this proposition plus the propositions presupposed in C (excluding those that are consequences of the presupposed propositions by themselves).

7.2 Challenges to the Traditional Conception

7.21 *Demonstratives: A Revision of Kaplan*

The first challenge is to develop a proper semantic account of demonstratives. In section 4.35, I noted the consequences of certain differences between *pure indexicals* and *demonstratives* for

---

[3] Grice (1967) and chapter 9 of Soames (2003b), See Bach (1999) for a critique of Grice on conventional implicature.
[4] Grice allows for the possibility that there might be other, nonconversational, nonconventional implicatures due to other maxims, including considerations of politeness. See Grice (1967), p. 28.

Kaplan's twin goals of developing indexical logic and giving the semantics of English indexicals. Since the semantic content of a pure indexical α is an objective feature of a context C that is fully determined by applying its meaning to C, (i) α's referent at C doesn't depend on special referential intentions of the speaker, (ii) different occurrences of α must have the same content at C, and (iii) the formal evaluation of sentences containing α can proceed without interference from hidden or variable factors. By contrast, since the content of a demonstrative is *not* fully determined by applying its meaning to C, it lacks features (i)–(iii), which are crucial to Kaplan's logic.[5] This is what led him to regiment (replace) pairs consisting of a simple demonstrative d, plus a demonstration δ, by the term $\ulcorner$dthat (the x: Dx)$\urcorner$ in which the content of $\ulcorner$the x: Dx$\urcorner$ incorporates that of δ. Although this is acceptable for regimenting indexical reasoning, it does not provide an acceptable semantic account of English demonstratives.

As shown in Salmon (2002), the most straightforward projection of Kaplan's formal language onto English replaces complex 'dthat'-terms with corresponding complexes combining an English demonstrative d with a nonlinguistic demonstration δ (speaker intention, gesture, etc.). Just as $\ulcorner$dthat (the x: Dx)$\urcorner$ is a singular term for Kaplan, so d + δ is treated as a complex singular term, and hence a grammatical constituent of English. It is, of course, odd to treat nonlinguistic entities as expressions. However, the crucial defect of this idea is that it treats demonstratives like 'she' and 'this' on the model of 'dthat'—which is not itself a meaning or reference-bearing constituent, but rather a syncategorematic part of larger "expressions" that are.[6] Since demonstratives

---

[5] See Bach (2005) for an interesting take on the significance of the fact that demonstratives lack (i)–(iii).

[6] If 'dthat' had a meaning, yielding contents in contexts, its content in C would be a function—either (i) from the referent of $\ulcorner$the x: Dx$\urcorner$ at C and world-state w, to itself, which would become the referent of $\ulcorner$dthat (the x: Dx)$\urcorner$ at C,w, or (ii) from the content of $\ulcorner$the x: Dx$\urcorner$ at C to its referent at C, Cw, which is the referent of $\ulcorner$dthat (the x: Dx)$\urcorner$ at C,w. (i) is incompatible with the rigidity of 'dthat'-terms, and thus ruled out. (ii) is incompatible with direct referentiality of $\ulcorner$dthat (the x: Dx)$\urcorner$—since its content in C

do have meanings, contents, and referents (in contexts), they can't be analyzed on this model.

Salmon's solution adds demonstrations to contexts (rather than to sentences). In addition to a time, world-state, agent, and place, some contexts now include demonstrations indexed to occurrences of demonstratives—the ith occurrence of a demonstrative in a sentence being assigned the ith demonstration in the context. As with Kaplan, demonstrations—including referential intentions and pointings—have contents, and determine referents. The content of an occurrence of 'that' at C is the referent, at C, of the demonstration provided for it, if there is such a referent; otherwise the occurrence has no content at C. Similarly for occurrences of 'she', except that the referent of the demonstration must be female. The content of an occurrence of a complex demonstrative ⌜that F⌝ at C is the unique referent, at C, of the corresponding demonstration, provided that F applies to it; otherwise it has no content at C. All occurrences of demonstratives are directly referential.

This conservative modification of Kaplan is both consistent with the traditional thesis (1) relating semantic content to assertion, and a reasonable candidate for being semantically correct. However, it does raise serious worries.

(i) Demonstratives have context-invariant meanings mastered by competent speakers. For Salmon, however, demonstrative *words* don't have fixed characters, or contents in contexts. Only their *occurrences* in sentences do—with different occurrences of the same word assigned different contents at *some* contexts. So, if meanings are characters, Salmon's demonstratives don't have meanings. Are they exceptions, or *are* meanings never characters?

---

would be a complex consisting of the content of 'dthat' plus the *content* of the description (instead of being the referent of the description at C). *So,* 'dthat' lacks reference and semantic content itself, but has a systematic effect on the reference and contents of larger expressions containing it. Analogous conclusions would apply to 'she', 'this', etc., if they were treated like 'dthat'. See Salmon (2002).

(ii) Demonstrations are obscure in both Salmon and Kaplan. Sometimes it is hard to identify any demonstration—as when I utter ⌜He is F⌝ knowing that something special about the situation will make it clear who I am talking about, even though I don't do anything to identify him. What is *the demonstration* in this case? Is it an artifact of the theory that whatever determines a *speaker's* reference has to be regarded as a *thing* belonging to the same class as the actions we ordinarily call 'demonstrations'? Is it also an artifact that this thing is seen as playing a role in determining *semantic content* (at a context)?

(iii) Whatever demonstrations are, Salmon requires them to determine unique referents, even when F in ⌜that F⌝ is rich enough to do so itself, or with only minimal contextual supplementation. Why? Is it because he is using "demonstrations" to cover whatever it is that is needed for *de re* thought about an object, and so to guarantee the direct referentiality of demonstratives?[7]

(iv) Questions also arise for obvious demonstrations like gestures. Along with descriptions, they are thought to have contents that determine referents—perhaps along the lines: *the thing pointed at/intended by the speaker.* How does this fit with Salmon's adoption of Kaplan's overall framework, which allows sentences to express propositions in contexts in which the agent isn't speaking or thinking at all? Are we to allow contexts in which no one demonstrates anything to contain "demonstrations"? Although "demonstrations" in such contexts might be contents of qualitative descriptions 'the thing that appears such and such from here', such demonstrations aren't operative in real speech situations—if speaker-hearers are supposed to grasp

---

[7] For a different treatment of complex demonstratives, challenging the thesis that they are directly referential terms, see King (2001). That thesis, which has since become controversial, is debated in Salmon (2008) and King (2008).

the thing demonstrated by entertaining the demonstration. For although different conversational participants may converge on the same referent, they needn't use the same content to identify it.

The first of these worries results from trying to combine a *semantic theory* that takes meanings to be characters with a *logic of demonstratives* that must allow different occurrences of demonstratives to have different contents in the same context. Since these goals conflict, something has to be given up. The other worries arise from a failure to clarify precisely what role demonstrations are supposed to play. Salmon's primary concern is, I think, the use of language in thought. When one uses a demonstrative, one typically *has an object in mind*. On this picture, demonstrations may be whatever allow one to have *de re* thoughts about objects—in which case paradigms of them aren't public gestures, but (perhaps) something like private referential intentions. But language is also used to communicate. From this perspective, gestures that contribute to the contents of assertions and other speech acts *are* paradigms of demonstrations. These acts are more than hints about what is asserted; their contribution to the *warrant* required for holding the speaker responsible for the truth of a particular content is partly constitutive of what is asserted. When demonstrations aren't needed for this purpose, as in (ii) and (iii) above, they are dispensable. Although theorists tend to focus on one or the other of these paradigms—private thought vs. public communication—it is better to think of semantics as being neutral between them. Shortly, I will sketch a conception of semantics, and role for indexicals, that is.

7.22 *Incomplete Descriptions, Quantifiers, and Context*

The problem posed by sentences containing incomplete definite descriptions is that those who assertively utter them often succeed in saying something true, without saying anything untrue—despite the fact that the semantic content of the sentence uttered appears to be untrue (because the description fails to denote an object uniquely).

2. I parked *the car* behind some cars across the street.

Given that this content is untrue, one needs to explain both how something else gets asserted, and why, even if it does, the semantic content of the sentence uttered isn't also asserted. Such sentences create a *prima facie* conflict between the traditional connection, (1), between meaning and assertion, and an otherwise well-supported analysis of descriptions.

For a time, many attempted to resolve the conflict by positing semantically referential readings of descriptions in which ⌜the F⌝ is, like ⌜this F⌝, a directly referential term denoting a contextually salient object that satisfies F.[8] On this story, when I use (2) to talk about a particular car c, the proposition *that I parked c behind some cars across the street* is both (2)'s semantic content in the context, and also the proposition I use (2) to assert. Presupposing the traditional thesis (1), proponents of this analysis essentially read their semantic conclusion off pragmatic facts about assertion. This was a mistake, both because (1) itself requires empirical support, and because the semantically referential analysis of descriptions is incorrect, as shown in Kripke (1979b), Salmon (1982), Neale (1990, 1993), and Soames (1986, 1994b, 2005b, 2009c).

However, it is not a mistake to suppose that one who utters (2) may assert *that c is parked behind some cars across the street.* The traditional account can explain why this is asserted, and also why the claim *that the (unique) car (in the domain of discourse) that is parked behind some cars across the street* isn't asserted—even if it is (2)'s semantic content. Since the domain contains several cars, the description, 'the car', fails to denote anything, and the semantic content of (2) is transparently untrue. If, as we may assume, the speaker is observing the maxim not to assert obvious untruths, the normal presumption that the semantic content of the sentence uttered is asserted will be defeated, and a pragmatic reconstrual of the remark will be required. When it is clear that the speaker is talking about c, the speaker will be taken to assert *that c is parked behind some cars across the street.*

[8] See Donnellan (1966, 1978), Wettstein (1981), and Barwise and Perry (1983).

However, not all cases are so easy. In a situation in which I know that you saw me speaking to a student s in my office this morning, I may assertively utter

3. The student I spoke to in my office this morning wants to go to graduate school.

when I see you in the afternoon, thereby saying something true about s, without saying anything untrue—even if I spoke to other students after s left (and you realize that I had other meetings, but don't know whether they involved students). In such a case, there is no presumption that the domain of discourse at the time of utterance includes only one student, and no commitment arising from my utterance that it does. As long as we both know that I am using the description to talk about s, I may succeed in telling you that s wants to go to graduate school, without saying anything untrue. If—as the traditional thesis (1) maintains—there is normally a presumption that the semantic content of the sentence uttered is asserted, then, in this case, it is *not* defeated. Consequently, either the semantic content of (3) *in this context* doesn't require me to have spoken to a unique student in my office this morning, or we have a counterexample to (1).

Later, I will defend the second alternative. Here, I present an argument for the first given in Stanley (2000, 2002), and Stanley and Szabo (2000).[9] For these authors, the domains of *occurrences* of quantifier phrases, including definite descriptions, vary from context to context—and in some contexts different *occurrences* of the same quantifier may be assigned different domains. The question at issue is whether this should be viewed as pragmatic enrichment of a fixed semantic content, or as a case of contextually varying semantic contents, including varying semantic contents of different occurrences of a quantifier within the same context. A key example is (4), which can be used to say something true—e.g., the proposition expressed by (5)—and nothing untrue, despite the fact that some student somewhere fails to answer some question or other.

---

[9] See Bach (2000) and Neale (2000a) for critiques.

4. Every student answered every question.

5. Every student *in this class* answered every question *on his/her exam.*

In Stanley (2000) it is argued that this can be explained only as the contextual interpretation of a hidden variable in the logical form (6) of (4) restricting the range of the second quantifier. (We ignore supplementation of the first quantifier.)

6. [Every x: Student x] [Every y: Question y & f(x) y] x answered y

According to this view, the context of utterance C supplies the interpretation of 'f'—assigning it a function from individuals x to the property *being on x's exam* (which is predicated of y). As a result, for each student x, the range of the second quantifier is restricted to questions on x's exam, and the semantic content of (4) in C is, we may suppose, proposition (5). Stanley claims that since the proposition that (4) is used to assert can arise only from taking an occurrence of 'x' to be bound by the first quantifier, and assigning 'f' (which operates on 'x') a value, these variables must be present in logical form. On this view, the value assigned to 'f' is its *semantic* content in C, just as the values assigned to demonstratives by demonstrations are their contents, on Salmon's story.

Since, on Stanley's proposal, hidden occurrences of variables in logical form always accompany occurrences of nouns, (3_1) is said to be the logical form of (3).

3_1. [the x: student x & I spoke to x in my office this morning x, & f(x) x] x wants to go to graduate school.

Here, f is assigned the function that assigns to any argument the property: *being identical with s.* As a result, the semantic content of (3) in C is identified with the proposition asserted by my utterance of it, which, in turn, is taken to be (roughly) the (true) proposition *that the student, s, to whom I spoke in my office this morning wants to go to graduate school.* On this analysis, the traditional thesis (1) is preserved. Our next question will be whether it should be.

7.23 *Pragmatic Enrichment and Incomplete Semantic Contents*

7.231 IMPLICATURE, IMPLICITURE, AND ASSERTION

The term "conversational impliciture," coined in Bach (1994), covers cases in which what the speaker implicitly says in uttering S is a conversational enrichment of the semantic content of S (in the context).[10] Bach distinguishes two conceptually different cases of this phenomenon, represented by (7) and (8).

7a. The lamp is cheap. (for a Tiffany)
 b. Strom is too old. (to be a good senator)
 c. Brian is ready. (to get down to work)
 d. Jane is coming. (to the party)
 e. Al has finished. (eating dinner)
8a. You're not going to die. (of that paper cut)
 b. I haven't eaten dinner. (today)
 c. John has three cars. (exactly)
 d. I have nothing to wear. (appropriate)
 e. Everyone is asleep. (there)

Although the sentences in (7) are grammatically well formed, their semantic contents each lack an element that must be supplied pragmatically to generate a complete, truth-evaluable, proposition (or, as he puts it, "to complete the proposition radical"). For example, 'ready' expresses a relation between agents and events, actions, or tasks, while 'finish' expresses a relation an agent bears to a task or activity (or, in some cases, to something intimately related to a task or activity, as in 'He finished the sandwich'). Although most semantically 2-place predicates require the second argument place to be syntactically filled—compare (7e) with the ungrammatical *'Al has completed'—some, like 'ready' and 'finish', don't. Thus, one who utters (7c) or (7e) relies on contextually shared assumptions to fill out what proposition is asserted. If Bach is right, these cases are counterexamples to thesis (1).

---

[10] See also Sperber and Wilson (1986), Carston (1988, 2002), and Recanati (1989, 1993) for the related notion of a conversational *explicature*.

According to him, (8a–e) are too, though for a different reason. He takes (8a–e) to express complete propositions, but ones which, nevertheless, are often not among the propositions asserted, communicated, or meant by a speaker who utters them. The propositions *implicitly asserted* in his scenarios are that you aren't going to die *from that cut,* that I haven't eaten dinner *today,* that John has *exactly* three cars, that I have nothing *appropriate* to wear, and that everyone *there* is asleep. It is less clear which propositions are supposed to be semantically expressed. He seems to take them to be equivalent to the propositions expressed by (9a–e), without constituents corresponding to the italicized expressions.

9a. You're not going to die *ever.*
  b. I haven't *ever* eaten dinner.
  c. John has *at least* three cars.
  d. I have nothing *whatsoever* to wear.
  e. Everyone *in the entire universe* is asleep.

Here, pragmatic enrichment is taken to *expand* the complete propositions asserted by utterances of the sentences in (8) by adding constituents to yield the contextually desired assertive contents.

Though the analysis of (7) is plausible, the account of (8) is more controversial.[11] One bone of contention is whether the semantic contents of (8d,e) are, like their counterparts (9d,e), context-invariant, as opposed to context-sensitive, as Stanley and Szabo maintain. A different issue is whether examples like (8c), as well, perhaps, as the others, express *complete, truth evaluable* propositions. In Soames (2008c) it is argued that bare numerical quantifiers, ⌜n Fs⌝, have semantic contents that are neutral between different possible contextual completions—⌜at least/exactly/at most/. . . n Fs⌝. For example, it is shown that, depending on context, (10a) can be used to assert any of an indefinite range of propositions illustrated by (10b).

10a. Matriculated students may take five courses.

---

[11] See, however, Cappelen and Lepore (2005), who take (7a–e) to express complete, context-invariant propositions.

b. Matriculated students may take *at least/exactly/at most/up to/from a contextually determined k up to* five courses.

Since positing multiple, open-ended ambiguity (plus indexicality) is unattractive, it is argued that the semantic content of (10a) is indeterminate, and in need of pragmatic completion.

On this view, the bare numerical quantifier occurring in

11. I have n Fs.

can be syntactically expanded in several ways: e.g., *at least n, exactly n, up to n, at most n, up to n but more than m*. While the contents of these completions are possible pragmatic enrichments of the semantic content of the quantifier, the content of (11) is free of any such completion, and so is nonspecific. What is asserted by a normal, literal use of a sentence S is constrained to be an obvious and relevant enrichment of the semantic content of S. When this content is a complete, truth-evaluable proposition, that proposition may count as one of its own possible enrichments. When it isn't, as in (11), nonvacuous enrichment is required for a proposition to be asserted. Either way, the semantic content of S can be taken to be (or to impose) a set of constraints on what one literally says or asserts in uttering S. When these fail to determine a complete proposition, pragmatic enrichment is required. When they do determine a complete proposition, it is optional. If the option is taken, the semantic content of S is asserted only when it is an obvious and relevant consequence of the enriched proposition that it is the speaker's primary intention to assert (plus relevant background assumptions).

Pragmatic enrichments of utterances in communicative situations are influenced by many factors, including the purpose and direction of the conversation, remarks previously made, contextually salient information, shared background assumptions, and Gricean maxims. In addition to generating conversational implicatures, over and above what is asserted, the maxims help determine what an utterance asserts by narrowing the class of possible enrichments to those that advance the conversation. When several enrichments are otherwise feasible, the maxims direct one to select the most informative, relevant proposition for which one has adequate evidence. In so doing, the maxims play a role in determining what is asserted, and so contribute to the truth conditions of utterances.[12]

7.232 PERVASIVE INCOMPLETENESS? POSSESSIVES, COMPOUND NOMINALS, AND TEMPORAL MODIFICATION

Temporal modification fits the same pattern.

> 12a. The philosopher, David Lewis, is dead.
>   b. The deceased philosopher, David Lewis, was a metaphysician.

'Dead' and 'deceased' apply to someone x at time t only if x lived, and so existed, before t, but no longer does; 'philosopher' and 'metaphysician' apply to x at t only if x does philosophy and metaphysics at t—both of which require existence at t.[13] Assume further that the descriptions in (12) quantify over a domain including individuals who once existed, but no longer do. Under these assumptions, it is plausible that the propositions asserted by utterances of (12a,b) arise from their semantic contents by contextually inserting temporal indicators of some sort into the contents of the descriptions—even though these indicators are not syntactically represented in the sentences themselves. Taking the form of the copula to represent time or tense, we may represent the semantic contents of (12a,b) as equivalent to the following.

> S12a. [the x: x be a philosopher & x be David Lewis] x *is* dead
> S12b. [the x: x be deceased & x be a philosopher & x be David Lewis] x *was* a metaphysician

---

[12] Pragmatic enrichments also occur in thought, though the reasons for them—which centrally involve the automatic assumptions of the agent—are different from those that occur in conversation.

[13] When used as adjectives modifying N, 'dead' and 'deceased' combine with N to form a complex predicate true of o at t iff before t, o was alive and satisfied N, but at t, o no longer exists.

Although the descriptions lack temporal indicators, it is clear what needs to be added. Utterances of (12a) and (12b) assert the contents roughly indicated by (A12a) and (A12b).

A12a. [the x: x *was* a philosopher & x was David Lewis] x *is* dead

A12b. [the x: x *is* deceased & x *was* a philosopher & x was David Lewis] x *was* a metaphysician

In these cases, the semantic content of the description lacks temporal specification, which must be added pragmatically before one has a candidate for assertion. Although speaker-hearers can choose which specification to supply, the meanings of 'dead' and 'deceased' leave few options. In other cases, different choices are possible in different contexts. For example, if

13. The owner of the Harrison Street house is temporarily away on business.

is uttered shortly after the house has burned down, what is asserted is that the person who, *in the past*, owned the Harrison Street house is temporarily away. In other contexts, what is asserted is that the person who *presently* owns the house is away. Thus, even though its semantic content, which is expressed by (S13), is temporally incomplete, (13) can be used to assert either proposition (A13a) or proposition (A13b).

S13. [the x: x own the house on Harrison St.] temporarily x is away on business

A13a. [the x: x *owned* the house on Harrison St.] temporarily x is away on business

A13b. [the x: x *owns* the house on Harrison St.] temporarily x is away on business

Possessive noun phrases, which in English come in various forms—⌐NP's N⌐, ⌐the N of NP⌐, ⌐an N of NP's⌐—provide similar results. Since the first, prenominal, form is the freest (compare 'today's meeting' with *'the meeting of today'), I will concentrate on it. The point at issue involves the relation holding between the referent of what is, grammatically, the possessor NP and the individual that ⌜NP's N⌝ is used by the speaker to designate. There are two ideal types of utterance involving such noun phrases to consider. In the first, N provides a clear default choice R for the crucial relation, nothing in the context overrides that choice, and R is a constituent of the assertive content of an utterance of a sentence containing the possessive noun phrase. In the second case, either the default choice provided by N is pragmatically overridden in favor of a pragmatically determined relation R*, or there is no clear default choice to begin with, and the relation is only minimally constrained by the semantic content of N. In both of these sub-cases, the speaker relies heavily on pragmatic supplementation to provide assertable content. Between these two ideal types there is a continuum of cases running from those in which very little in the way of special contextual stage setting is needed to determine the relevant relation to those in which such stage setting does virtually all the work.

Examples of the first type involve a relational noun N that expresses, or is defined in terms of, a 2-place relation R from which the default relation required by the possessive noun phrase is determinable. In the case of 'Tom's teacher' R is the relation a teacher bears to his or her student, while in the case of 'Tom's student' it is the converse of that relation. Variations on this theme include 'Tom's mother', 'Tom's boss', 'Tom's leg', and 'Tom's birthplace'. For a case in which there is a default choice, but it is pragmatically overridden, imagine that two journalists, Tom and Bill, have been assigned to go to a local school and to interview one student each. When this is both salient and presupposed in a conversation, one can use 'Tom's student' to refer to the student *interviewed by* Tom, and 'Bill's student' to refer to the one *interviewed by* Bill. Here the relation that shows up in the assertive content of one's utterance is pragmatically determined to be the relation that an interviewer bears to one he or she interviews. Similar scenarios can be imagined for uses of 'Tom's teacher', 'Tom's mother', and 'Tom's boss'.

Pragmatic supplementation is also evident in uses of possessive noun phrases involving nonrelational nouns, like 'car' and 'book', to which a potential "possessor" may bear various relations. For example, 'Tom's car' can be used to talk about a car he owns, drives, has rented, is riding in, will leave in, or has bet on in the Indianapolis 500—while 'Pam's book' may be used to talk about a book she wrote, plans to write, is reading, owns, has edited, or has requested from the library. *This isn't ambiguity; it is incompleteness, or nonspecificity.* The semantic content of ⌜NP's N⌝ requires that which it is used to designate to be something to which N applies that bears a relation R to the denotation of the possessor NP. However, in these cases, it is clear that the semantic content of the possessive noun phrase does not determine the identity of R, but at most constrains it. Thus, the semantic contents of sentences containing such possessives require pragmatic enrichment in order to generate complete propositions that are candidates for assertion.[14]

The picture extends to compound nominals ⌜$N_1 N_2$⌝, which apply to things satisfying N_2 that have something to do with—i.e., bear some relation R to—what satisfies N_1. In cases like 'philosophy department', 'pig farm', and 'bus terminal' the identity of R is pretty clear. Notice, though, how the relation R varies in 'sugar pill' (pill *made of* sugar), 'vitamin pill' (pill *containing* vitamins), 'diet pill' (pill *one takes as part of* a diet), 'pain pill' (pill *to alleviate* pain), and 'sleeping pill' (pill *to induce* sleep). With so much variation, there is no simple, general rule specifying the interpretation of ⌜$N_1 N_2$⌝ as a compositional function of the interpretations of its constituents. This variation is, of course, not itself a counterexample to the thesis that the semantic content of a phrase is a compositional function of the semantic contents of its parts. However, if one insists that the semantic contents of these expressions be complete, full-fledged constituents of the propositions *asserted* by utterances of sentences containing them, then the semantic rules for computing their contents will be complex and highly idiosyncratic.

[14] See Barker (1995, 2008) for informative and detailed empirical discussion of possessives.

If, on the other hand, the semantic contents of compound nominals merely constrain R, without always determining it, then the semantic theory can be simplified by relying on pragmatic enrichment to complete the job. The appeal of this idea is enhanced by contexts in which the nominals take on unusual assertive contents. We are all familiar with the fact that 'brick warehouse' can be used to talk either about a warehouse made of bricks, or a warehouse for storing bricks. We wouldn't normally say the same about 'sugar warehouse', 'marshmallow warehouse', or 'paper warehouse' because we wouldn't normally think of warehouses made of these materials. But we can easily imagine scenarios in which such structures are denoted by utterances of these nominals. Thus, either the nominals have been ambiguous all along, having meanings they have seldom, if ever, been used to express, or their semantic contents can be pragmatically enriched in new ways when unusual contexts are encountered.

Other examples of unusual interpretations made to fit unusual situations involve nominals such as 'laughter pill' and 'truth session'. Though these are seldom, if ever, used, we can imagine scenarios in which the first is used to talk about pills that cause/prevent/increase the volume of/decrease the volume of one's laughter, and the second is used to talk about sessions in which one is expected to tell the truth about oneself/one is expected to tell the truth about one's coworkers/one learns to detect when others are telling the truth/one is required to pledge allegiance to the regime's version of the truth/one studies different philosophical conceptions of truth. These examples fit the semantic incompleteness-pragmatic enrichment thesis, but not the ambiguity thesis. One could maintain, in response, that the semantic content of $\ulcorner N_1 N_2 \urcorner$ always expresses the same complete, but utterly minimal, content as $\ulcorner N_2$ that bears some relation or other to $N_1 \urcorner$ (in which case, the semantic content of $\ulcorner$That is an $N_1 N_2 \urcorner$ would be trivially true and that of $\ulcorner$That isn't an $N_1 N_2 \urcorner$ would be trivially false whenever the N_2 applied to referent of 'that'). But then, since pragmatic enrichment would always be needed to get from semantic to assertive content, thesis (1) would have to be rejected anyway. Once it is, there is no point in insisting that semantic contents must always be complete.

7.3 A New Conception of the Relationship between Meaning, Thought, Assertion, and Implicature

7.31 *The Guiding Principle*

The examples in the previous section suggest a new account of the connection between the meaning of S and its use in thought and assertion.[15]

> 14. The meaning M of a sentence S is (or imposes) a set of constraints on what normal, literal uses of S (without conversational implicatures that force reinterpretation) assert, or express. When S contains indexicals, or is otherwise semantically incomplete (e.g., lacks any syntactic representation of some semantically required element), M will not determine a complete proposition by itself, and so must be pragmatically supplemented in order for a use of S to express a complete thought, or result in a truth-evaluable assertion. When M does determine a complete proposition p, normal, literal uses of S express thoughts, or result in assertions, the contents of which are proper pragmatic enrichments of p. In such cases, p itself counts as asserted (or entertained in thought) only if p is an obvious, relevant, and apriori consequence of the enriched proposition(s) asserted (entertained) in uttering S (or using it privately), together with background presuppositions at the time of use (which, in the case of utterances, must be shared by conversational participants).[16]

I will first use (14) to revisit demonstratives and incomplete descriptions, and then apply it to well-known problems involving names and propositional attitudes.

---

[15] Different, but related, alternatives to the traditional connection between meaning and assertion (and semantics and pragmatics generally) are given in Sperber and Wilson (1986), Recanati (1989, 1993), Carston (2002), and Neale (2005). Soames (2008c) includes remarks comparing these to the approach given here. See King and Stanley (2005) for a contrasting view.

[16] When S semantically expresses a complete proposition, it may count as a proper pragmatic enrichment of itself.

7.32 *Demonstratives and Incomplete Descriptions Revisited*

According to (14), the meaning of an expression *constrains* its contributions to the assertions made, and thoughts expressed, by uses of sentences containing it, without always fully determining them. Demonstratives fit this conception. The referent of an occurrence of 'he' is constrained to be male, the referent of an occurrence of 'she' must be female, the referent of an occurrence of 'now' is a stretch of time including the present moment, the referent of an occurrence 'we' is a group containing the agent, and the referent of an occurrence of ⌜that F⌝ is something that satisfies F.[17] To know the meanings of these terms is to know these constraints, and to know that one uses the terms to *say of* their referents that they are so and so. Everything else used to fill out the referents of such occurrences in contexts, and their contributions to assertions, or thoughts they are used to express, is pragmatic.[18]

This approach has advantages over Salmon's revision of Kaplan. Since it doesn't require a complete, semantically determined proposition for every felicitous use of a sentence, no difficulty is created by the fact that different occurrences of the same demonstrative can be used to refer to different things in the same context, and so make different contributions to the proposition asserted, or expressed, by an utterance. The same point applies to pure indexicals. Although assertive utterances always last less than a day, and are seldom joint actions, these are merely contingent, non-semantic facts. It is easy to imagine two people—x and y—jointly uttering "He was rude. First, he insulted *me* and then he insulted *me*"—with all the words said in unison, except for the two occurrences of 'me', which are pronounced singly by x and y, respectively. This joint utterance results in a joint assertion to which the two occurrences of 'me' make different contributions.

---

[17] There are, of course, extended uses of some of these demonstratives, as when one refers to a ship as 'she' even though the ship isn't female, or says of one's favorite team, 'We won the game' even though one is not on the team.

[18] See section 9.4 of Bach (1987) for an early statement of this basic view.

Similar scenarios can be imagined involving two occurrences of 'today' in a long utterance. On Salmon's version of Kaplan, these examples preclude taking characters to be meanings to purely indexical *words*, just as characters are precluded from being the meanings of demonstrative *words* and *phrases*. But surely, it is precisely words and phrases (rather than their occurrences) that have meaning. This is no problem for (14).

Thesis (14) also dispenses with so-called "demonstrations." This is a plus, since the term is typically applied to very different things—including whatever determines the subjects of the *de re* thoughts one uses sentences containing demonstratives to express, reference-determining intentions in communicative acts, like assertion, and gestures providing warrant for hearers' inferences about the targets of the speaker's predications. Though each has a role to play in the use of language, knowledge of these roles isn't knowledge of meaning.

Now for incomplete descriptions. The problem they posed stemmed from an incorrect conception, (1), of the relationship between meaning and assertion. When (1) is replaced by (14), the data fall into place. Consider again the case in which I assertively utter (3) to inform you about a certain student s, to whom you know I spoke.

3. The student I spoke to in my office this morning wants to go to graduate school.

Although (3) semantically expresses the complete proposition expressed by (3S), the fact that we both know that I am talking about s results in the assertion of the pragmatically enriched proposition (3A)—*that the student, s, I spoke to in my office this morning wants to go to graduate school.*

3S. [the x: student x & I spoke to x in my office this morning x] x wants to go to graduate school.
3A. [the x: student x & I spoke to x in my office this morning x, & x = s] x wants to go to graduate school.

The proposition I assert is true, even if the semantic content of the sentence I use to do so is untrue (because I spoke to several students). Among the obvious consequences of my remark that

I am also counted as asserting are *that s wants to go to graduate school* and *that a student I spoke to in my office this morning wants to go to graduate school*. However, since it is not presupposed *that I spoke to one and only one student in my office this morning* or *that s = the (unique) student I spoke to in my office this morning*, proposition (3S) isn't a consequence of my remark, and so isn't asserted. Thus, I use a sentence containing an incomplete definite description to say something true, and nothing untrue. This is the paradigm for explaining all similar cases.

Does it extend to the example in which (4) is used to assert proposition (5)?

4. Every student answered every question.
5. Every student *in this class* answered every question *on his/her exam.*

The argument that it doesn't depends on the contention that what needs to be added to (4) to get the proposition expressed by (5) *is not an independent propositional constituent*, but rather something that interacts semantically with an operator that is already syntactically represented.

> Since the supposed unarticulated constituent [what needs to be added to get the content of (5) from (4)] is not the value of anything in the sentence uttered, *there should be no readings of the relevant linguistic constructions in which the unarticulated constituent varies with the values introduced by operators in the sentence uttered.* Operators in a sentence can only interact with variables in the sentence that lie within their scope. . . . Thus . . . [the] interpretation [of the unarticulated constituent] cannot be controlled by operators in the sentence.[19]

The point seems to be that what needs to be added to (4) to get (5) is not a single semantic value, but a formula, 'is on x's exam', the semantic value of which varies with different assignments to 'x'. Because of this, Stanley thinks, pragmatic enrichment can't

---

[19] Stanley (2000), pp. 410–11, my emphasis. (As before, we ignore enrichment of the first quantifier in (4)).

result from enriching a constituent of proposition (4S), which is the semantic content of (4) on the pragmatic-enrichment account.

4S. [Every x: Student x] [Every y: Question y] x answered y

Thus, he assumes, if pragmatic enrichment were to occur, it would have to involve adding *extra words* to interact with those already there. After arguing against this, he concludes that since enrichment of (4) can't explain its use to assert proposition (5), (4) must have a hidden variable in logical form requiring contextual interpretation. And if this is true of (4), it is also true of (3).

But the argument doesn't work; it is perfectly possible to arrive at proposition (5) by pragmatically enriching proposition (4S). On the Frege-Russell analysis of quantification, the latter is a complex in which the higher-order property *being instantiated by every student* is predicated of *being one who answered every question*. Pragmatic enrichment involves replacing the latter property with an enriched version of it: *being one who answered every question on one's exam*. No new words are introduced; we simply have an operation on contents. Thus, Stanley's variable-binding argument has no force against the view at which it is aimed.

By itself, this doesn't show that the pragmatic treatment of incomplete descriptions is superior to the contextually semantic approach. However, it opens the door to general arguments for this conclusion. If, as I believe, our previous arguments show that the traditional connection between meaning and assertion must be abandoned in favor of the new conception, then the pragmatic account of incomplete descriptions has the advantage of not requiring any additional complications to account for the data. Since the hidden variables posited by the semantic approach, plus the new parameter added to contexts to evaluate them, are just such complications, they should be avoided unless independent arguments based on other data show them to be needed.[20] The semantic approach also inserts hidden variables into every quantifier phrase *no matter how much the quantifier has already been*

[20] The reader should check Stanley (2000, 2002) and Stanley and Szabo (2000) to evaluate the case on this point.

restricted by linguistic material already there. Isn't this redundant? If a long restricting clause appearing overtly on the quantifier completely determines its range, the hidden variable will be inert. So why posit it?[21]

Finally, troubling questions are raised by (what I take to be) our best conception of natural-language semantics. On that conception, contexts are real situations in which agents use words; the semantic contents of sentences are constraints on use, knowledge of which (together with knowledge of conversational maxims, presuppositions, and other contextually salient facts) would allow a rational agent to reliably identify the propositions sentences are used to assert, or otherwise express. According to the hidden-variable analysis such contexts must supply functions from individuals to *properties meant by speakers* as values of (occurrences of) such variables. Since any difference in the functions supplied signals a difference in the contexts supplying them, it is a consequence of this view that in order to find out what the context is for a speaker's remark, one *first* must find out *what the speaker is saying.* This reverses the proper order of explanation, in which knowledge of semantic information is one ingredient in explaining knowledge of what is said, rather than the other way around.[22] No such reversal plagues the pragmatic treatment of incomplete descriptions (or of simple and complex demonstratives).

7.33 *Names and Propositional Attitudes*

In exploring pragmatic enrichment involving names, it is useful to begin with partially descriptive names, such as 'Lake Washington'.[23] To be a competent user of the name, one must know that to assertively utter $\ulcorner$Lake Washington is F$\urcorner$ is to say of the referent that it is a lake with the property expressed by F. One must also have acquired a referential intention that picks out the

---

[21] A version of this point is made in Bach (2000).

[22] For similar arguments against treating speaker intentions as contextual semantic parameters, see Bach, "Why Speaker Intentions Are Not Part of Context," unpublished but available at http://online.sfsu.edu/~kbach.

[23] See chapter 5 of Soames (2002), and Soames (2005c).

right body of water—often by acquiring the name from others, and intending to use it as they do. Typically, competent users associate the name with extra information, as well—which varies greatly from speaker to speaker. Thus, although most users have extra information about the lake, little, if any, of it is common to them all. Consequently, the meaning of the name is, roughly, that of the description 'the x: x is a lake & x = y', relative to an assignment to 'y' of the body of water standing at the end of a chain of uses of the name. The guiding ideas are (i) that the meaning of an expression is what it contributes to the meanings of sentences in which it occurs, and (ii) that the meaning of S is what is common to what is asserted or expressed by all normal, literal uses of S.[24] On this view, the semantic content of ⌜Lake Washington is F⌝ is a singular proposition that predicates the property *being a lake that is $\mathscr{F}$* of the lake itself.

Next consider the name, 'Carl Hempel', which refers to a former philosopher of science. Uses of it are often pragmatically enriched. When you ask, "Which Princeton philosophers were your neighbors?" and I answer, "Carl Hempel was my neighbor," I assert that the Princeton philosopher, Carl Hempel, was my neighbor. What *I* mean by *this use* of the name is roughly what 'the Princeton philosopher, Carl Hempel' means. But this isn't what the name itself means. Different speakers who use it to refer to the same man associate it with different information. Because of this, different uses of ⌜Carl Hempel was F⌝ may result in different assertions, due to different pragmatic enrichments. Since there is little or no content common to these enrichments, the semantic content of the name (the common assertive contribution it makes

---

[24] There are two different, but equivalent, ways of characterizing the meaning of S: (a) as a set of constraints on what normal, literal uses assert (or express), and (b) as what is common to what is asserted (or expressed) by such uses. Taking (a) as primary, the common element required is that all the asserted (expressed) contents satisfy the constraints. Taking (b) as primary, the common element can be thought of as a skeleton underlying all the asserted (expressed) contents, while the constraints in (a) specify that what is asserted (expressed) must be an enrichment, of a specified sort, of the common element.

in all relevant contexts) is just its referent. The same is true of 'Peter Hempel', which is what Mr. Hempel's friends used to call him. Hence, the two names have the same semantic content, as do (15a) and (15b), even though utterances of them nearly always assert or convey different information.[25]

15a. Peter Hempel was Carl Hempel.
  b. Carl Hempel was Carl Hempel.

This illustrates an important point about linguistic meaning. The claim that S means (semantically expresses) p is a *theoretical* claim about the *common content* of what is asserted, or expressed, by uses of S in different contexts. When ordinary speakers (including many philosophers and linguists) are asked what sentences mean, they often don't address this question. Instead they focus on what *they* would use the sentences to assert or express, or what information *they* would gather from uses of them.[26] They focus on what they would mean or assert in particular cases, rather than on what the sentences mean in the common language. The latter is the notion needed in semantics. This is the sense in which (15a) and (15b) have the same meaning; the information *invariantly* contributed to what is asserted or expressed by different normal uses is the same for both. This is compatible with the fact that in nearly all contexts they would be used to assert or express different things.

The semantic content of (15a,b) is the proposition expressed by (S15a,b), relative to an assignment of Mr. Hempel to 'x' and 'y'.

S15a,b. In the past, $x = y$

In a context in which it is presupposed that 'Carl Hempel' names a well-known philosopher, and 'Peter Hempel' names my neighbor, my utterance of (15a) asserts the proposition, (A15a), *that my neighbor Peter Hempel was the philosopher Carl Hempel* (where m is Mr. Hempel).

---

[25] Soames (2002), chapter 3.
[26] See pp. 67–72 of Soames (2002), also Soames (2005d), and section 6 of Bach (2005).

A15a. In the past, [the x: x was my neighbor & x = m] =
[the y: y was a philosopher & y = m]

This proposition is a pragmatic enrichment of the semantic content of (15a). Since this assertion wouldn't be made using (15b), substitution of terms with the same semantic content changes assertion potential while preserving linguistic meaning. This illustrates how a proper conception of the relationship between semantics and pragmatics can contribute to the solution of what have seemed to be intractable problems. Linguistically simple names have a Millian semantics, and a partially descriptive pragmatics of assertion. Thus, although Kripke was right that the *meanings* of these names are thoroughly nondescriptive, Frege was right that we often *use* sentences containing them to make assertions, and express beliefs, that are at least partially descriptive.[27]

7.4 What Is Meaning? The Distinction between Semantics and Pragmatics

The arguments given for the new account of the relationship between semantic content, thought, and assertion are based on a wide variety of linguistic constructions, expressions, and sentence types. In each case, a conclusion is drawn about what parts of the information carried by utterances are included in the semantic contents of the sentences uttered, and what parts arise pragmatically, from the use of sentences. These conclusions are not things about which we have reliable intuitions simply by understanding the language. Speakers are mostly reliable judges of what *they*, as well as others, mean, assert, and convey by particular utterances. But they aren't able to reliably distinguish information contributed by sentence meaning from that added pragmatically. The right conception of meaning should explain why this is.

Semantic and pragmatic theories are rational reconstructions of the ability of speaker-hearers to interpret uses of sentences. In

---

[27] Lessons for Frege's Puzzle, Kripke's Puzzle, and related issues are drawn in Soames (2002, 2005c, 2005d, 2009c).

cases of assertion, they draw on a pool of contextually shared information to identify certain propositions as asserted, and others as implicated. The cognitive processes by which this occurs are not our concern.[28] We can, however, construct an idealized model, many of the inputs and outputs of which correspond to those of the real cognitive processes. In the model, the sentence uttered is paired with the semantic content assigned to it by our semantic theory. Idealized speaker-hearers extract information from the pair using conversational maxims, plus propositions representing common conversational knowledge. Conclusions about what is asserted, conveyed, and implicated are rationally inferred. The model is validated by showing that its conclusions match those of real speakers.

When we show that some proposition p conveyed by an utterance can be generated by the pattern of reasoning characterizing conversational implicature, we show that p is rationally extractable from the utterance, together with a defensibly austere conception of meaning, whether or not real speakers consciously, or unconsciously, follow this route. What guides us is a conception of linguistic meaning as *least common denominator*. The meaning of an expression is the minimal content that must be associated with it by a rational agent—over and above the agent's ability to reason intelligently and efficiently—in order to communicate with other members of the linguistic community. The point is not heuristic, but constitutive. This is what meaning is. No matter what idiosyncratic processes speaker-hearers actually go through in interpreting utterances, the question of what part of that which is asserted or conveyed is due to meaning, and what part is due to pragmatic factors, is determined by rational reconstruction, not psycholinguistic research.

On this view, it is an open question—not to be prejudged one way or the other—what role semantic contents play in our cognitive lives. It is not assumed that speaking a common language requires us to have psychologically robust representations that carry all and only the information *semantically* encoded by sentences. What is required is that there be a substantial core of information

---

[28] They also weren't Grice's concern. For useful discussion, see Saul (2002).

that nearly all of us extract from utterances in various contexts. The meaning of S is an abstraction from this common core. It is that which is both common to what literal uses of S assert or express in all normal contexts, and what an ideally rational agent would have to master—over and above the ability to reason intelligently, and engage in cooperative social behavior—in order to communicate using S with other speakers.[29]

Selected Further Reading

Bach, Kent (1994), "Conversational Impliciture."

Barker, Chris (1995), *Possessive Descriptions.*

Carston, Robyn (2002), *Thoughts and Utterances.*

Grice, Paul (1967) "Logic and Conversation."

King, Jeffrey C., and Jason Stanley (2005), "Semantics, Pragmatics, and the Role of Semantic Content," in Szabo (2005).

Neale, Stephen (2005) "Pragmatism and Binding."

Recanati, F. (1989), "The Pragmatics of What is Said."

Salmon, Nathan (2002), "Demonstrating and Necessity."

Soames, Scott (2002), *Beyond Rigidity*, chapters 3, 5, and 8.

—— (2008c), "Drawing the Line between Meaning and Implicature—and Relating Both to Assertion."

—— (2009c) "The Gap between Meaning and Assertion: Why What We Literally Say Often Differs from What Our Words Literally Mean."

Sperber, Dan, and Deirdre Wilson (1986), *Relevance.*

Stanley, Jason (2000), "Context and Logical Form."

---

[29] When a piece of information M is the meaning of S, both ideal agents and ordinary speakers will, in some way, associate M with S. Nevertheless, ordinary speakers may fail to recognize M as the meaning of S, because their competence with S doesn't require any psychologically significant distinction between M and other, nonsemantic, information they associate with S. See Soames (2005d, 2009c, and chapter 3 of 2002).

References

Adams, Robert

(1974), "Theories of Actuality," *Noûs* 8: 211–31.

Bach, Kent

(1987), *Thought and Reference*, Oxford: Oxford University Press.

(1994), "Conversational Implicature," *Mind and Language* 9: 124–62.

(1999), "The Myth of Conventional Implicature," *Linguistics and Philosophy* 22: 367–421.

(2000), "Quantification, Qualification, and Context," *Mind and Language* 15: 262–83.

(2005), "Context *ex Machina*," in Szabo (2005).

Barker, Chris

(1995), *Possessive Descriptions*, Stanford, CA: Center for the Study of Language and Information.

(2008), "Possessives and Relational Nouns," in Claudia Maienborn, Klaus von Heusinger, and Paul Portner, eds., *Semantics: An International Handbook of Natural Language Meaning,* Berlin: de Gruyter.

Barwise, Jon, and John Perry

(1983), *Situation Semantics*, Cambridge, MA: MIT Press.

Beaney, Michael

(1996), *Making Sense*, London: Duckworth.

Bennett, Jonathan

(2003), *A Philosophical Guide to Conditionals*, Oxford: Clarendon Press.

Berger, Alan

(2002), *Terms and Truth*, Cambridge, MA: MIT Press.

Burgess, John

(1998), "Quinus ab omni naevo vindicatus," in Ali Kazmi, ed., *Meaning and Reference, Canadian Journal of Philosophy Supplement,* vol. 23, 25–65.

(1999), "Which Modal Logic Is the Right One?" *Notre Dame Journal of Formal Logic* 40: 81–93; reprinted in Burgess, *Mathematics, Models, and Modality*, Cambridge: Cambridge University Press, 2008.

(2009), *Philosophical Logic*, Princeton and Oxford: Princeton University Press.

References

Cappelen, Herman, and Ernest Lepore
(2005), *Insensitive Semantics*, Oxford: Blackwell.

Carnap, Rudolf
(1936), "Wahrheit und Bewährung," *Acts du Congres International de Philosophie Scientifique*, Paris; trans. as "Truth and Confirmation," in H. Feigl and W. S. Sellars, eds., *Readings in Philosophical Analysis*, New York: Appleton-Century-Crofts, 1949.
(1942), *Introduction to Semantics*, Cambridge: Harvard University Press.
(1947), *Meaning and Necessity*, Chicago: University of Chicago Press; second, expanded edition, 1956.
(1949), "Truth and Confirmation," in H. Feigl and W. S. Sellars, eds., *Readings in Philosophical Analysis*, New York: Appleton-Century-Crofts.
(1963), "Intellectual Autobiography," in P. A. Schilpp, ed., *The Philosophy of Rudolf Carnap*, LaSalle, IL: Open Court.

Carston, Robyn
(1988), "Implicature, Explicature, and Truth-Theoretic Semantics," in R. M. Kempson. ed., *Mental Representations: The Interface between Language and Reality*, Cambridge: Cambridge University Press.
(2002), *Thoughts and Utterances*, Blackwell: Oxford.

Chalmers, David
(2002), "On Sense and Intension," in James Tomberlin, ed., *Philosophical Perspectives* 16: 135–82.

Chomsky, Noam
(1965), *Aspects of a Theory of Syntax*, Cambridge, MA: MIT Press.

Church, Alonzo
(1944), *Introduction to Mathematical Logic*, Princeton: Princeton University Press.
(1954), "Intentional Isomorphism and the Identity of Belief," *Philosophical Studies* 5: 65–73.

Davidson, Donald
(1967), "Truth and Meaning," *Synthese* 17: 304–23; reprinted in Davidson (2001).
(1970), "Semantics for Natural Language," Bruno Visentini et al., ed., *Linguaggi nella società e nella tecnica*, Milan: Edizioni di Comunità; reprinted in Davidson (2001).

(1976), "Reply to Foster," in Gareth Evans and John McDowell, eds., *Truth and Meaning*, Oxford: Clarendon Press, 33–41; reprinted in Davidson (2001).

(1977), "Reality without Reference," *Dialectica* 31: 247–53; reprinted in Davidson (2001).

(1990), "The Structure and Content of Truth," *Journal of Philosophy* 87: 279–328.

(2001), *Inquiries into Truth and Interpretation*, Oxford: Clarendon Press.

Donnellan, Keith

(1966), "Reference and Definite Descriptions," *Philosophical Review* 75: 281–304.

(1977), "The Contingent Apriori and Rigid Designators," *Midwest Studies in Philosophy* 2: 12–27.

(1978), "Speaker Reference, Descriptions, and Anaphora," in Peter Cole, ed., *Syntax and Semantics, 9: Pragmatics*, New York: Academic Press; reprinted in French, Uehling, and Wettstein (1979).

Dowty, Robert, Robert Wall, and Stanley Peters

(1981), *Introduction to Montague Semantics*, Dordrecht: Reidel.

Dummett, Michael

(1973), *Frege's Philosophy of Language*, London: Duckworth.

Edgington, Dorothy

(2004), "Counterfactuals and the Benefit of Hindsight," in P. Dowe and P. Noordhof, eds., *Causation and Counterfactuals*, London: Routledge.

Etchemendy, John

(1988), "Tarski on Truth and Logical Consequence," *Journal of Symbolic Logic* 53: 51–79.

[Fara], Delia Graff

(2001), "Descriptions as Predicates," *Philosophical Studies* 102: 1–42.

Field, Hartry

(1972), "Tarski's Theory of Truth," *Journal of Philosophy* 69: 347–75.

Foster, John

(1976), "Meaning and Truth Theory," in Gareth Evans and John McDowell, eds., *Truth and Meaning*, Oxford: Clarendon Press.

Frege, Gottlob

(1879), *Begriffsschrift*, Halle: Louis Nebert; trans. by S. Bauer-Mengelberg, in J. van Heijenoort, ed., *From Frege to Gödel*, Cambridge, MA: Harvard, 1967.

References

(1891), "Function und Begriff," address given to the *Jenaische Gesellschaft für Medicin und Naturwissenschaft*, January 9, 1891, Jena; trans. by Peter Geach as "Function and Concept," in Geach and Black (1970).

(1892a), "Uber Sinn and Bedeutung," *Zeitschrift für Philosophie und philosophische Kritik* 100: 25–50; trans. by Max Black as "On Sense and Reference," in Geach and Black (1970).

(1892b), "On Concept and Object," first published in the *Vierteljahrsschrift für wissenschaftliche Philosophie* 16, 192–205; trans. by Peter Geach, in Geach and Black (1970).

(1893, 1903), *Grundgesetze der Arithmetik*, vol. 1, 1893; vol. 2, 1903, Jena; trans. by M. Furth as *The Basic Laws of Arithmetic*, Berkeley and Los Angeles: University of California Press, 1964.

(1918), "Der Gedanke," *Beitrage zur Philosophie des deutschen Idealismus* 1; trans. by A. Quinton and M. Quinton as "The Thought," *Mind* 65 (1956): 289–311.

French, Peter, Theordore Uehling, and Howard Wettstein, eds.

(1979), *Contemporary Perspectives in the Philosophy of Language*, Minneapolis: University of Minnesota Press.

Geach, Peter, and Max Black

(1970), *Translations from the Philosophical Writings of Gottlob Frege*, Oxford: Blackwell.

Gomez-Torrente, Mario

(1996), "Tarski on Logical Consequence," *Notre Dame Journal of Formal Logic* 37: 125–51.

Goodman, Nelson

(1947), "The Problem of Counterfactual Conditionals," *Journal of Philosophy* 44: 113–28.

(1955), *Fact, Fiction, and Forecast*, Indianapolis: Bobbs-Merrill.

Grice, Paul

(1967), "Logic and Conversation," William James lectures at Harvard University; reprinted in *Studies in the Way of Words*, Cambridge, MA: Harvard University Press.

Harman, Gilbert

(1972), "Deep Structure as Logical Form," in Donald Davidson and Gilbert Harman, eds., *Semantics of Natural Language*, Dordrecht: Reidel.

(1977), "How to Use Propositions," *American Philosophical Quarterly* 14: 173–76.

Harper, W. L., R. Stalnaker, and G. Pearce
(1981), *If's*, Dordrecht: Reidel, 1981.

Hawthorne, John, and David Manley
(forthcoming), *The Reference Book*.

Heim, Irene
(1982), *The Semantics of Definite and Indefinite Noun Phrases*, Ph.D. thesis, University of Massachusetts, Amherst.

Higginbotham, James
(1992), "Truth and Understanding," *Philosophical Studies* 65: 3–16.

Jackson, Frank
(1987), *Conditionals*, Oxford: Blackwell.
(1998a), *From Metaphysics to Ethics*, Oxford: Clarendon Press.
(1998b), "Reference and Description Revisited," *Philosophical Perspectives* 12: 201–18.

Jeshion, Robin
(2001), "Acquaintanceless *De Re* Belief," in M. J. O'Rourke, et al., eds., *Truth and Meaning: Investigations in Philosophical Semantics*, New York: Seven Bridges Press.

Kamp, Hans
(1981), "A Theory of Truth and Semantic Representation," in J.A.G. Groenendijk, T.M.V. Janssen, and M.B.J. Stokhof, eds., *Formal Methods in the Study of Language*, Mathematical Centre Tracts 135, Amsterdam.
(1995), Discourse Representation Theory," in J. Verschueren, J.-O. Östman, and J. Blommaert, eds., *Handbook of Pragmatics*, Amsterdam: Benjamins.

Kaplan, David
(1968), "Quantifying In," *Synthese* 19: 178–214.
(1970), "What Is Russell's Theory of Descriptions?" in Wolfgang Yourgrau and Allen D. Breck, eds., *Physics, Logic, and History*, New York: Plenum; reprinted in David F. Pears, ed., *Bertrand Russell: A Collection of Critical Essays*, New York: Anchor Books, 1972.
(1986), "Opacity," in Lewis E. Hahn and Paul A. Schilpp, eds., *The Philosophy of W. V. Quine*, La Salle, IL: Open Court.
(1989a), "Demonstratives: An Essay on the Semantics, Logic, Metaphysics and Epistemology of Demonstratives and Other Indexicals," in Joseph Almog, John Perry, and Howard Wettstein, eds., *Themes from Kaplan*, New York: Oxford University Press.

References

(1989b), "Afterthoughts," in Joseph Almog, John Perry, and Howard Wettstein, eds., *Themes from Kaplan*, New York: Oxford University Press.

King, Jeffrey C.

(2001), *Complex Demonstratives*, Cambridge, MA: MIT Press.

(2007), *The Nature and Structure of Content*, Oxford: Oxford University Press.

(2008), "Complex Demonstratives, QI Uses, and Direct Reference," *Philosophical Review* 117: 99–117.

King, Jeffrey C., and Jason Stanley

(2005), "Semantics, Pragmatics, and the Role of Semantic Content," in Szabo (2005).

Kment, Boris

(2006), "Counterfactuals and Explanation," *Mind* 115: 261–310.

Kripke, Saul

(1958), "A Completeness Theorem in Modal Logic, *Journal of Symbolic Logic* 24: 1–14.

(1963a), "Semantical Analysis of Modal Logic," *Zeitschrift für mathematische Logik und Grundlagen der Mathematik* 9: 67–96.

(1963b), "Semantical Considerations on Modal Logic," *Acta Philosophica Fennica* 16: 83–94.

(1972), "Naming and Necessity," in Donald Davidson and Gilbert Harman, eds., *Semantics of Natural Languages*, Dordrecht: Reidel; reissued as *Naming and Necessity*, Cambridge, MA: Harvard University Press, 1980.

(1979a), "A Puzzle about Belief," in A. Margalit, ed., *Meaning and Use*, Dordrecht: Reidel.

(1979b), "Speaker's Reference and Semantic Reference," in French, Uehling, and Wettstein (1979).

(2005), "Russell's Notion of Scope," *Mind* 114: 1005–1037.

(2008), "Frege's Theory of Sense and Reference," *Theoria* 74: 181–218.

Kroon, Frederick

(1987), "Causal Descriptivism," *Australasian Journal of Philosophy* 65: 1–17.

Larson, Richard, and Gabriel Segal

(1995), *Knowledge of Language*, Cambridge, MA: MIT Press.

Lepore, Ernest, and Kirk Ludwig

(2007), *Donald Davidson: Meaning, Truth, Language and Reality*, New York: Oxford University Press.

(2009), *Donald Davidson's Truth-Theoretic Semantics*, New York: Oxford University Press.

Lewis, David

(1973a), *Counterfactuals*, Cambridge, MA: Harvard University Press.

(1973b), "Causation," *Journal of Philosophy* 70: 556–67.

(1979), "Possible Worlds," in *Loux* (1979).

(1986), *On the Plurality of Worlds*, Oxford: Blackwell.

(1997), "Naming the Colors," *Australasian Journal of Philosophy* 75: 325–42.

(2000), "Causation as Influence," *Journal of Philosophy* 97: 182–97.

(2001), *The Plurality of Worlds*, Oxford: Wiley-Blackwell.

(2004), "Causation as Influence," in J. Collins, E. Hall, and L. Paul, eds., *Causation and Counterfactuals*, Cambridge, MA: MIT Press.

Lewis, C. I., and C. H. Langford

(1932), *Symbolic Logic*, New York: Dover.

Loux, Michael J., ed.

(1979), *The Possible and the Actual*, Ithaca and London: Cornell University Press.

Montague, Richard

(1970), "English as a Formal Language," in Bruno Visentini et al., eds., *Linguaggi nella società e nella tecnica*, Milan: Edizioni di Comunità; reprinted in Thomason (1974).

(1973), "The Proper Treatment of Quantification in Ordinary English," in J. Hintikka and J. Moravcsik, eds., *Approaches to Natural Language*, Dordrecht: Reidel; reprinted in Thomason (1974).

Neale, Stephen

(1990), *Descriptions*, Cambridge, MA: MIT Press.

(1993), "Grammatical Form, Logical Form, and Incomplete Symbols," in A. D. Irvine and G. A. Wedeking, eds., *Russell and Analytic Philosophy*, Toronto: Toronto University Press.

(2000a), "On Being Explicit," *Mind and Language* 15: 284–94.

(2000b), "On a Milestone of Empiricism," in P. Kotatko and A. Orenstein, eds., *Knowledge, Language, and Logic: Questions for Quine*, Dordrecht: Kluwer.

(2005), "Pragmatism and Binding," in Szabo (2005).

Nolan, Daniel

(1997), "Impossible Worlds: A Modest Approach," *Notre Dame Journal of Formal Logic* 38: 535–73.

References

Partee, Barbara

(2004), *Compositionality in Formal Semantics: Selected Papers*, Oxford: Blackwell.

Perry, John

(1977), "Frege on Demonstratives," *Philosophical Review* 86: 474–97.

Putnam, Hilary

(1970), "Is Semantics Possible?" *Metaphilosophy* 1: 187–201; reprinted in Hilary Putnam, *Philosophical Papers*, vol. 2, Cambridge: Cambridge University Press, 1975.

(1973), "Explanation and Reference," in G. Pearce and P. Maynard, eds., *Conceptual Change*, Dordrecht: Reidel; reprinted in Putnam, *Philosophical Papers*, vol. 2, Cambridge: Cambridge University Press, 1975.

(1975), "The Meaning of 'Meaning'," in K. Gunderson, ed., *Language, Mind, and Knowledge*, Minnesota Studies in the Philosophy of Science, vol. 7, Minneapolis: University of Minnesota Press; reprinted in Putnam, *Philosophical Papers*, vol. 2, Cambridge: Cambridge University Press, 1975.

Quine, W. V.

(1943), "Notes on Existence and Necessity," *Journal of Philosophy* 40: 113–27.

(1947), "The Problem of Interpreting Modal Logic," *Journal of Symbolic Logic* 12: 43–48.

(1951), "Two Dogmas of Empiricism," *Philosophical Review* 60: 20–43.

(1953), "Reference and Modality," in *From a Logical Point of View*, Cambridge, MA: Harvard University Press.

(1960), *Word and Object*, Cambridge, MA: MIT Press.

Recanati, F.

(1989), "The Pragmatics of What Is Said," *Mind and Language* 4: 97–120.

(1993), Direct Reference, Oxford: Blackwell.

Richard, Mark

(1993), "Articulated Terms," *Philosophical Perspectives* 7: 207–30.

Rosen, Gideon

(1990), "Modal Fictionalism," *Mind* 99: 327–52.

Russell, Bertrand

(1903), *Principles of Mathematics*, New York: Norton.

(1905), "On Denoting," Mind 14: 479–93.

(1910–11), "Knowledge by Acquaintance and Knowledge by Description," *Proceedings of the Aristotelian Society* 11: 108–28.

Sainsbury, Mark

(1979), *Russell*, London: Routledge.

Salmon, Nathan

(1981), *Reference and Essence*, Princeton: Princeton University Press.

(1982), "Assertion and Incomplete Definite Descriptions," *Philosophical Studies* 42: 37–45.

(1984), *Frege's Puzzle*, Cambridge, MA: MIT Press.

(1987), "Existence," in James Tomberlin, ed., *Philosophical Perspectives* 1: 49–108.

(1988), "How to Measure the Standard Metre," *Proceedings of the Aristotelian* Society 88: 193–217.

(1989), "On the Logic of What Might Have Been," *Philosophical Review* 98: 3–34.

(1998), "Nonexistence," *Noûs* 32: 277–319.

(2002), "Demonstrating and Necessity," *Philosophical Review* 111: 497–537.

(2005), "On Designating," *Mind* 114, 1069–1133.

(2006), "A Theory of Bondage," *Philosophical Review* 15: 415–48.

(2008), "That F," *Philosophical Studies* 141: 263–80.

Saul, Jennifer

(2002), "What Is Said and Psychological Reality: Grice's Project and Relevance Theorists' Criticisms," *Linguistics and Philosophy* 25: 347–72.

Schaffer, Jonathan

(2004), "Counterfactuals, Causal Independence and Conceptual Circularity," *Analysis* 64: 299–309.

Searle, John

(1983), *Intentionality*, Cambridge: Cambridge University Press.

Soames, Scott

(1984), "What Is a Theory of Truth?" *Journal of Philosophy* 81: 411–29; reprinted in Soames (2009b).

(1986), "Incomplete Definite Descriptions," *Notre Dame Journal of Formal Logic* 27: 349–75; reprinted in Soames (2009a).

(1987), "Direct Reference, Propositional Attitudes, and Semantic Content," *Philosophical Topics* 15: 44–87; reprinted in Soames (2009b).

(1989), "Semantics and Semantic Competence," *Philosophical Perspectives* 3: 575–96; reprinted in Soames (2009a).

(1992), "Truth, Meaning, and Understanding," *Philosophical Studies* 65: 17–35; reprinted in Soames (2009a).

References

(1994a), "Attitudes and Anaphora," in James Tomberlin, ed., *Philosophical Perspectives* 8: 251–72; reprinted in Soames (2009b).

(1994b), "Donnellan's Referential/Attributive Distinction," *Philosophical Studies* 73: 149–68; reprinted in Soames (2009a).

(1999a), *Understanding Truth*, New York: Oxford University Press.

(1999b), "The Indeterminacy of Translation and the Inscrutability of Reference," *Canadian Journal of Philosophy* 29: 321–70.

(2002), *Beyond Rigidity*, New York: Oxford University Press.

(2003a), *Philosophical Analysis in the Twentieth Century*, vol. 1: *The Dawn of Analysis*, Princeton: Princeton University Press.

(2003b), *Philosophical Analysis in the Twentieth Century*, vol. 2: *The Age of Meaning*, Princeton: Princeton University Press.

(2003c), "Understanding Deflationism," in John Hawthorne and Dean Zimmerman, eds., *Philosophical Perspectives* 17: 369–83; reprinted in Soames (2009b).

(2005a), *Reference and Description*, Princeton: Princeton University Press.

(2005b), "Why Incomplete Descriptions Do Not Defeat Russell's Theory of Descriptions," *Teorema* 24: 7–30; reprinted in Soames (2009a).

(2005c), "Beyond Rigidity: Reply to McKinsey," *Canadian Journal of Philosophy* 35: 169–78.

(2005d), "Naming and Asserting," in Szabo (2005); reprinted in Soames (2009a).

(2006), "The Philosophical Significance of the Kripkean Necessary Aposteriori," in Ernest Sosa and Enrique Villanueva, eds., *Philosophical Issues* 16: 288–309; reprinted in Soames (2009b).

(2007a), "Actually," in Mark Kalderon, ed., *Proceedings of the Aristotelian Society*, supplementary volume 81, 251–77; reprinted in Soames (2009b).

(2007b), "The Substance and Significance of the Dispute over Two-Dimensionalism," *Philosophical Books* 48: 34–49.

(2008a), "Truth and Meaning: In Perspective," in Peter French and Howard Wettstein, eds., *Midwest Studies in Philosophy* 32: 1–19; reprinted in Soames (2009a).

(2008b), "Why Propositions Can't Be Sets of Truth-Supporting Circumstances," *Journal of Philosophical Logic* 37: 267–76; reprinted in Soames (2009b).

(2008c), "Drawing the Line Between Meaning and Implicature—and Relating Both to Assertion," *Noûs* 42: 529–54; reprinted in Soames (2009a).

(2009a), *Philosophical Essays*, vol. 1: *Natural Language: What It Means and How We Use It*, Princeton and Oxford: Princeton University Press.

(2009b), *Philosophical Essays*, vol. 2: *The Philosophical Significance of Language*, Princeton and Oxford: Princeton University Press.

(2009c), "The Gap between Meaning and Assertion: Why What We Literally Say Often Differs from What Our Words Literally Mean," in Soames (2009a).

(2010), *What Is Meaning?* Princeton: Princeton University Press.

(forthcoming a), "Kripke on Epistemic and Metaphysical Possibility: Two Routes to the Necessary Aposteriori," in Alan Berger and Saul Kripke, Cambridge: Cambridge University Press.

(forthcoming b), "What Are Natural Kinds?" *Philosophical Topics* 35: 329–42, 2007.

(forthcoming c), "Propositions," in Delia Fara Graff and Gillian Russell, eds., *Companion to the Philosophy of Language*, New York: Routledge.

Sosa, Ernest

(1970), "Propositional Attitudes *De Dicto* and *De Re*," *Journal of Philosophy* 67: 883–96.

Sperber, Dan, and Deirdre Wilson

(1986), *Relevance*, Cambridge, MA: Harvard University Press.

Stalnaker, Robert

(1968), "A Theory of Conditionals," in *Studies in Logical Theory*, American Philosophical Quarterly Monograph Series, no. 2, Oxford: Blackwell; reprinted in Harper, Stalnaker, and Pearce (1981).

(1975), "Indicative Conditionals," *Philosophia* 5: 269–86.

(1976), "Possible Worlds," *Noûs* 10: 65–75; reprinted in Loux (1979).

(1981a), "A Defense of Conditional Excluded Middle," in Harper, Stalnaker, and Pearce (1981).

(1981b), Indexical Belief," *Synthese* 49: 129–51; reprinted in Stalnaker (1999).

(1984), Inquiry, Cambridge, MA: MIT Press.

(1999), Context and Content, Oxford: Oxford University Press.

Stalnaker, Robert, and Richmond Thomason

(1973), "A Semantic Theory of Adverbs," *Linguistic Inquiry* 4: 195–220.

References

Stanley, Jason

(2000), "Context and Logical Form," *Linguistics and Philosophy* 23: 391–434.

(2002), "Making it Articulated," *Mind and Language* 17: 149–68.

Stanley, Jason, and Zoltan Gendler Szabo

(2000), "On Quantifier Domain Restriction," *Mind and Language* 15: 219–61.

Szabo, Zoltan Gendler

(2005), *Semantics versus Pragmatics,* Oxford: Oxford University Press.

Tarski, Alfred

(1935), "Der Wahrheitsbegriff in den formalisierten Sprachen," *Studia Philosophica,* vol. 1, 261–405; trans. as "The Concept of Truth in Formalized Languages," in Woodger (1956), 152–278.

(1936), "Über den Begriff der logischen Folgerung," *Acts du Congres International de Philosophie Scientifique,* 7 (Actualites Scientifiques et Industrielles, 394), Paris, 1–11; trans. as "On the Concept of Logical Consequence," in Woodger (1956), 409–20.

(1944), "The Semantic Conception of Truth," *Philosophy and Phenomenological Research* 4: 341–76.

(1969), "Truth and Proof," *Scientific American*, June, 63–67.

Thomason, Richmond

(1974), ed., *Formal Philosophy: Selected Papers of Richard Montague,* New Haven, CT: Yale University Press.

Wettstein, Howard

(1981), "Demonstrative Reference and Definite Descriptions," *Philosophical Studies* 40: 241–57.

Woodger, J. H.

(1956), *Truth, Semantics, Metamathematics*, Oxford: Oxford University Press; second edition, Indianapolis, IN: Hackett Publishing Company.

Index

Adams, Robert, 109
anaphoric pronouns, 17, 67, 70–71
apriority, 55, 77; and actuality, 132–34; and apriori consequence, 135–36; and contingency, 134–35; and epistemic possibility, 137–40; and singular propositions, 140–42

Bach, Kent, 147n3, 148n5, 153n9, 155–56, 164n18, 168nn21–22, 170n26
Barker, Chris, 161n14
Barwise, Jon, 112, 152n8
Bennett, Jonathan, 59n6
Berger, Alan, 87n8
Burgess, John, 54, 57n4

Cappelen, Herman, 156n11
Carnap, Rudolf, 2, 41–45, 124
Carston, Robyn, 155n10, 163n15
causation and counterfactual dependence, 60–61
Chalmers, David, 87n9
character (Kaplanian), 97, 101, 149, 151, 165
Chomsky, Noam, 45
Church, Alonzo, 42n13, 44n14
compositionality, 10–13, 20; and the Davidsonian project, 46–47; and Montague's treatment of natural languages, 64–65n9, 71; and pragmatic enrichment, 161
compound nominals, 161–62
conceivability and possibility, 53, 124
consequence, 131; logical, 33, 37–38, 102; apriori, 126–27, 132–33, 135–36
content, 1, 4, 8, 20, 97, 109, 111, 112, 114, 117; and assertion, 145, 147, 151–54; incomplete, 155–163; of indexicals and demonstratives, 96–103, 134,

148–51; mental, 18, 77, 118, 122; of names, 80, 83; of natural kind terms, 89–90; and pragmatic enrichment, 155–63, 165–73; and truth-theoretic semantics, 41–42, 45–46, 48; of variables, 134
context-invariance, 102–4, 149, 156, 170
conventional implicature, 147
conversational implicature, 146–47
conversational impliciture, 155–56

Davidson, Donald, 45–49, 56, 109, 111
definite descriptions, 9, 24–26; rigidified, 81–82, 99–100; scope of, 26–28; temporal enrichment of, 158–59
descriptivism about names, 77; strong version of, 80; weak version of, 81
direct reference, 97–99
Donnellan, Keith, 140, 152n8
Dowty, Robert, 71n14

Edgington, Dorothy, 59n6
essentialism, 53, 54, 55, 57–58, 77; and the necessary aposteriori, 91–93

Fara, Delia Graff, 25n7
Foster, John, 47
Frege, Gottlob, 1–2, 7–20, 43–44, 112–13, 115–16, 131, 167, 171
Frege's Puzzle, 8–11, 30–31, 83n7, 170–71

Goodman, Nelson, 57
Grice, Paul, 145–47, 172n28

Harman, Gilbert, 45n16, 142
Hawthorne, John, 142

Index

Higginbotham, James, 49n22
holism about meaning, 46

incomplete descriptions, 151–54, 165–68
indefinite descriptions, 24–25
indexicals, 19–20, 147–51, 164–65; logic of 93–94, 104–5; logical semantics of 94–97, 99–104
intensions, 43; and intensional isomorphism, 44; and intensional operators, 2, 16–17, 44, 67; and intensional transitives, 69, 71, 72; and the logic of demonstratives, 94

Jackson, Frank, 87n9
Jeshion, Robin, 142

Kaplan, David, 2, 19, 54, 77, 93–105, 140, 147–51
King, Jeff, 117, 146n1, 150n7, 163n15
Kment, Boris, 59–60
Kripke, Saul, 2, 15, 20, 28n10, 52n1, 54, 64, 73n16, 77–93, 101n20, 124, 131, 140–41, 152, 171
Kroon, Frederick, 87n9

Langford, C. H., 52n1
language of thought, 48–49
Larson, Richard, 48n21
Lepore, Ernest, 156n11
Lewis, C. I., 52n1
Lewis, David, 2, 52, 56–63, 87n9, 109, 110n2, 131
liar paradox, 33–34
logical form, 25–26

Manley, David, 142
meaning, 1–4, 7–10, 12; and common content, 170–71; in isolation, 25; as least common denominator, 172; relation to thought and assertion, 163–71; traditional conception of, 145–47; transparency/nontransparency of, 17–19, 77
modal argument, 81–83

modal logic, 50–53; interpretation of, 53–56
modal realism, 110
Montague, Richard, 2, 93
Montague semantics, 63–75

names, 9–10; fixing the reference of, 81, 83–88; logically proper, 29–30; and negative existentials, 30–33; and pragmatic enrichment, 168–71; as quantifiers, 67–70, 71–72, as rigid designators, 81
natural kind terms, 88–91; as rigid and nondescriptive, 90–91
Neale, Stephen, 26n8, 54n3, 152, 153n9, 163n15
Nolan, Daniel, 58n5

Partee, Barbara, 71n14
perception, 13, 90, 116–18, 141
Perry, John, 112, 152n8
Peters, Stanley, 71n14
possessive noun phrases, 159–61
pragmatic enrichment, 155–71
propositional attitude ascriptions, 2, 27, 116, 118–22, 168–71; and Frege's hierarchy, 13–14; and intensional semantics, 73; and pragmatic enrichment, 168–71; quantification into, 18–19, 29; and truth-conditional semantics, 111
propositional functions, 21–22
propositions, 3–4, 43–44, 109; cognitively real, 121–23; deflationary, 117–20; Frege-Russell, 113–16; need for, 111; as properties of making propositions true, 124; as representational, 114–17; as sets of world-states, 73, 112; singular, 18–20

quantification, 11, 20–23; bare nominal, 157–58; and context, 153–54, 166–67; and the modal *de re,* 54, 80; in Montague semantics, 65–68
Quine, W.V.O., 45–46, 54, 79

Recanati, F., 155n10, 163n15
reference transmission, 86–88; and
    natural kind terms, 90
Richard, Mark, 133n2
rigid designation, 15, 78–81, 97–99
Rosen, Gideon, 110n3
Russell, Bertrand, 2, 20–32, 112–13,
    121n13, 167

Salmon, Nathan, 28n10, 31n12, 55,
    64n9, 73n16, 93n16, 124, 129, 140,
    141n5, 148–52, 154, 164–65
Saul, Jennifer, 172n28
Schaffer, Jonathan, 59n6
Searle, John, 87n9
Segal, Gabriel, 48n21
semantic theories, 111; of counter-
    factual conditionals, 56–62; and
    demonstratives, 151; and the dis-
    tinction between semantics and
    pragmatics, 171–72; and possible
    worlds semantics, 55–56; and prag-
    matic enrichment, 162; and their
    relation to truth conditions, 43–44
Sosa, Ernest, 142
Sperber, Dan, 155n10, 163n15
Stalnaker, Robert, 2, 52n2, 56–63,
    71n13, 109, 111n4, 124–25, 131

Stanley, Jason, 153–54, 156, 163n15,
    166–67
state descriptions, 43; as sets of basic
    propositions, 124
Szabo, Zoltan Gendler, 153, 156,
    167n20

Tarski, Alfred, 2–3, 33–41, 131
tense and tense operators, 95, 158–59
Thomason, Richmond, 64n8, 71n13
truth, 33–49; arithmetical indefinabil-
    ity of, 36–37; and confirmation, 41;
    definition of, 34–36; gaps, 11, 12;
    and Gödel's incompleteness result,
    37; logical, 38, 43, 50–52, 54–55,
    102, 104; and meaning, 38–41, 42–
    43, 45–49, 73–75; in a model, 37–
    38; at a world, 50–51

Wall, Robert, 71n14
Wettstein, Howard, 152n8
Wilson, Dierdre, 155n10, 163n15
world states, 44, 52–53, 109–11; actual,
    50–51, 81–82, 96, 110; epistemically/
    metaphysically possible/impos-
    sible, 55–56, 124–25; knowledge of,
    126–28; nonexistent, 128–29; role
    in theories, 129–30